THE IMPORTANCE OF BEING EARNEST

A Trivial Comedy for Serious People

by Oscar Wilde

SAMUEL FRENCH

samuelfrench.co.uk

FOR AMATEUR PRODUCTION ENQUIRIES

UNITED KINGDOM AND WORLD
EXCLUDING NORTH AMERICA
plays@samuelfrench.co.uk
020 7255 4302/01

Each title is subject to availability from Samuel French,
depending upon country of performance.

THINKING ABOUT PERFORMING A SHOW?

There are thousands of plays and musicals available to perform from Samuel French right now, and applying for a licence is easier and more affordable than you might think

From classic plays to brand new musicals, from monologues to epic dramas, there are shows for everyone.

Plays and musicals are protected by copyright law, so if you want to perform them, the first thing you'll need is a licence. This simple process helps support the playwright by ensuring they get paid for their work and means that you'll have the documents you need to stage the show in public.

Not all our shows are available to perform all the time, so it's important to check and apply for a licence before you start rehearsals or commit to doing the show.

LEARN MORE & FIND THOUSANDS OF SHOWS

Browse our full range of plays and musicals, and find out more about how to license a show
www.samuelfrench.co.uk/perform

Talk to the friendly experts in our Licensing team for advice on choosing a show and help with licensing
plays@samuelfrench.co.uk   020 7387 9373

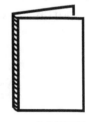

MUSIC USE NOTE

Licensees are solely responsible for obtaining formal written permission from copyright owners to use copyrighted music in the performance of this play and are strongly cautioned to do so. If no such permission is obtained by the licensee, then the licensee must use only original music that the licensee owns and controls. Licensees are solely responsible and liable for all music clearances and shall indemnify the copyright owners of the play(s) and their licensing agent, Samuel French, against any costs, expenses, losses and liabilities arising from the use of music by licensees. Please contact the appropriate music licensing authority in your territory for the rights to any incidental music.

IMPORTANT BILLING AND CREDIT REQUIREMENTS

If you have obtained performance rights to this title, please refer to your licensing agreement for important billing and credit requirements.

DRAMATIS PERSONAE

JOHN WORTHING, J.P.	Of the Manor House, Woolton, Hertfordshire
ALGERNON MONCRIEFF	His friend
REV. CANON CHASUBLE, D.D.	Rector of Woolton
MR GRIBSBY	Of the firm of Parker and Gribsby, Solicitors, London
MOULTON	Gardener
MERRIMAN	Butler to Mr Worthing
LANE	Mr Moncrieff's manservant
FOOTMAN	At the Manor House
LADY BRACKNELL	
HON. GWENDOLEN FAIRFAX	Her daughter
CECILY CARDEW	John Worthing's ward
MISS PRISM	Her governess

SCENES

ACT I   Algernon Moncrieff's rooms in Half Moon St. W.
ACT II   The garden at the Manor House, Woolton.
ACT III   Drawing-room at the Manor House, Woolton.
ACT IV   Same as ACT III.

Time:Summer, 1894

ACT I

SCENE: **ALGERNON**'s *rooms in Half Moon Street. Door upstage right and door left centre. Fireplace right centre. The room is luxuriously and artistically furnished.*

The sound of a piano is heard in the adjoining room. **LANE** *is arranging afternoon tea on the table, and after the music has ceased,* **ALGERNON** *enters.*

ALGERNON Did you hear what I was playing just now, Lane?

LANE I didn't think it polite to listen, sir.

ALGERNON I am sorry for that, for your sake. I don't play accurately—anyone can play accurately—but I play with wonderful expression. As far as the piano is concerned, sentiment is my forte. I keep science for Life.

LANE Yes, sir.

ALGERNON And, speaking of the science of Life, have you got the cucumber sandwiches cut for Lady Bracknell?

LANE Yes, sir.

ALGERNON Ahem! Where are they?

LANE Here, sir. *(Shows plate)*

ALGERNON *(takes one and eats it)* Oh! ...Lane, I see from your book that on Thursday night, when Lord Shoreham and Mr Worthing were dining with me, eight bottles of champagne are entered as having been consumed.

LANE Yes, sir. Eight bottles and a pint.

ALGERNON Why is it that at a bachelor's establishment the servants invariably drink the champagne? I ask merely for information.

LANE I attribute it to the superior quality of the wine, sir. I have often observed that in married households the champagne is rarely of a first-rate brand.

ALGERNON Good heavens! Is marriage so demoralizing as that?

LANE *(gravely)* I believe it is a very pleasant state, sir. I have had very little experience of it myself, up to the present. I have only been married once. That was in consequence of a misunderstanding between myself and a young person.

ALGERNON I don't know that I am much interested in your family life, Lane.

LANE No, sir, it is not a very interesting subject. I never think of it myself!

ALGERNON And very natural, I am sure... That will do, Lane, thank you!

LANE Thank you, sir.

False exit.

ALGERNON Ah! ...just give me another cucumber sandwich.

LANE Yes, sir. *(Returns and hands plate)*

Exit **LANE**.

ALGERNON Lane's views on marriage seem somewhat lax. Really, if the lower orders don't set us a good example—what on earth is the use of them? They seem as a class to have absolutely no sense of their moral responsibilities.

Enter **LANE**.

LANE Mr Ernest Worthing!

Exit.

Enter JACK.

ALGERNON How are you, my dear Ernest? What brings you to town?

JACK Oh, pleasure, pleasure! What else should bring one anywhere. *(Putting hand on* ALGERNON'*s shoulder)* Eating as usual, I see, Algy.

ALGERNON *(stiffly)* I believe it *is* customary to take some *slight* refreshment at five o'clock. Where have you been since last Thursday?

JACK *(sitting down)* Oh! in the country.

ALGERNON What on earth do you *do* there?

JACK *(pulling off his gloves)* When one is in town one amuses oneself. When one is in the country one amuses other people. It is excessively boring.

ALGERNON And who are the people you amuse?

JACK *(airily)* Oh! neighbours, neighbours!

ALGERNON Got nice neighbours in your part of Shropshire?

JACK Perfectly horrid. Never speak to one of them.

ALGERNON How immensely you must amuse them! *(Goes over and takes sandwich)* Shropshire is your county, Ernest, isn't it?

JACK *(going over to table)* Eh? ...Shropshire? ...Yes, of course. Hallo! Why all these cups? Why cucumber sandwiches? Who is coming to tea?

ALGERNON Oh! merely Aunt Augusta and Gwendolen.

JACK How perfectly delightful!

ALGERNON Yes, that is all very well; but I am afraid Aunt Augusta won't quite approve of your being here.

JACK May I ask why?

ALGERNON My dear fellow, the way you flirt with Gwendolen is perfectly disgraceful. It is almost as bad as the way Gwendolen flirts with you.

JACK I am in love with Gwendolen. I have come up to town expressly to propose to her.

ALGERNON I thought you had come up for pleasure... I call that business.

JACK How utterly unromantic you are!

ALGERNON I really don't see anything romantic in proposing. It is very romantic to be in love. But there is nothing romantic about a definite proposal. Why, one may be accepted. One usually is, I believe. Then the excitement is all over. The very essence of romance is uncertainty. If ever I get married, I'll certainly try to forget the fact.

JACK I have no doubt about that, dear Algy. The Divorce Court was specially invented for people whose memories are so peculiarly constituted.

ALGERNON Oh! there is no use speculating on that subject. Divorces are made in Heaven...please don't touch the cucumber sandwiches. They are ordered specially for Aunt Augusta. (*Takes one and eats it*)

JACK Well, you have been eating them all the time.

ALGERNON That is quite a different matter. She is my Aunt. Have some bread and butter. The bread and butter is for Gwendolen. Gwendolen is devoted to bread and butter.

JACK (*eating bread and butter*) And very good bread and butter it is, too.

ALGERNON Well, my dear fellow, you need not eat it all. You behave just as if you were married to her already. You are not married to her already, and I don't think you ever will be.

JACK Why on earth do you say that?

ALGERNON Well, in the first place, girls never marry the men they flirt with. Girls don't think it right.

JACK *(pulling himself together)* Oh! that is nonsense!

ALGERNON It isn't! It is a great truth. It accounts for the extraordinary number of bachelors that one sees all over town. In the second place, I don't give my consent.

JACK Your consent! What utter nonsense you talk!

ALGERNON My dear fellow, Gwendolen is my first cousin, and before I allow you to marry her, you will have to clear up the whole question of Cecily.

JACK Cecily! What on earth do you mean?

> ALGERNON *goes to bell and rings it. Then returns to tea-table and eats another sandwich.*

> What do you mean, Algy, by Cecily? I don't know anyone of the name of Cecily...as far as I remember.

Enter LANE.

ALGERNON Bring me that cigarette case Mr Worthing left in the hall the last time he dined here.

LANE Yes, sir.

Exit.

JACK Do you mean to say you have had my cigarette case all this time? I wish to goodness you had let me know. I have been writing frantic letters to Scotland Yard about it, I was very nearly offering a reward.

ALGERNON Well, I wish you would offer one. I happen to be more than usually hard up.

JACK There is no good offering a reward now that the thing is found.

Enter LANE, *with cigarette case on salver.* ALGERNON *takes it.* LANE *goes out.*

ALGERNON I must say, I think that is rather horrid of you, Ernest. *(Opens case and examines it)* However, it makes no matter; for now that I look at the inscription inside, I find that the thing isn't yours after all.

JACK *(irritably)* Of course it is mine. You have seen me with it a hundred times, and you have no right whatsoever to read what is written inside. It is a very ungentlemanly thing to read a private cigarette case.

ALGERNON Oh! it is absurd to have a hard and fast rule about what one should read and what one shouldn't. One should read everything. That is the true basis of modern culture. More than half of modern culture depends on what one shouldn't read.

JACK I am quite aware of that fact; and I don't propose to discuss modern culture. I simply want my cigarette case back.

ALGERNON Yes, but this isn't your cigarette case. This cigarette case is a present from someone of the name of Cecily, and you said you didn't know anyone of that name.

JACK I said I didn't remember knowing anyone of that name. I do remember now. She is my aunt.

ALGERNON Your aunt?

JACK Yes, charming old lady she is, too. Lives at Tunbridge Wells. Just give it back to me, Algy. *(Goes across stage to take it)*

ALGERNON *(retreating)* But why does she call herself little Cecily, if she is your aunt and lives at Tunbridge Wells? *(Reads)* "From little Cecily, with her fondest love."

JACK My dear fellow, what on earth is there in that? Some aunts are tall, some aunts are not tall. That is a matter that surely an aunt may be allowed to decide for herself. *You* seem to think that every aunt should be exactly like your aunt. That is absurd. For Heaven's sake give me back my cigarette case. *(Advances)*

ALGERNON *(sheltering himself behind table)* Yes, but why does your aunt call you her uncle? "From little Cecily with her fondest love to dear Uncle Jack." There is no objection I admit, to an aunt being a small aunt, but why an aunt, no matter what her size may be, should call her own nephew her uncle, I can't make out. Besides, your name isn't Jack at all. It is Ernest.

JACK It isn't Ernest—it's Jack.

ALGERNON You have always told me it was Ernest. I have introduced you to everyone as Ernest. You answer to the name of Ernest. You look as if your name was Ernest. It is perfectly absurd your saying that your name isn't Ernest. Why! it's on your cards. Here is one of them. "Mr Ernest Worthing, B.4, The Albany, W." Now I'll keep this as a proof that your name is Ernest, if you ever attempt to deny it, to me or to Gwendolen or to anybody else.

JACK Well, my name is Ernest in town and Jack in the country. And the cigarette case was given to me in the country.

ALGERNON Yes, but that does not account for the fact that your small aunt Cecily, who lives at Tunbridge Wells, calls you her dear uncle. Come, old boy, you had much better have the thing out at once.

JACK My dear Algy, you talk exactly as if you were a dentist. It is very vulgar to talk like a dentist when one isn't a dentist. It produces a false impression.

ALGERNON Well, that is exactly what dentists always do. Now go on: tell me the whole thing. I may mention that I have always suspected you of being a confirmed and secret Bunburyist; and I am quite sure of it now.

JACK What on earth do you mean by a Bunburyist?

ALGERNON I'll reveal to you the meaning of that incomparable expression as soon as you are kind enough to inform me why you are Ernest in town and Jack in the country.

JACK Well, produce my cigarette case first.

ALGERNON Here it is. *(Hands cigarette case)* Now produce your explanation; and pray make it remarkable.

JACK My dear fellow, there is nothing remarkable about this explanation at all. In fact it is perfectly ordinary. Old Mr Thomas Cardew, who adopted me when I was a little boy, under rather peculiar circumstances, and left me all the money I possess, made me in his will guardian to his grand-daughter Miss Cecily Cardew. Cecily, who addresses me as her uncle from motives of respect, resides at my place in the country under the charge of her admirable governess Miss Prism.

ALGERNON Where is that place in the country, by the way?

JACK That is nothing to you, dear boy. You are not going to be invited. I may tell you candidly that the place is not in Shropshire.

ALGERNON I suspected that, my dear fellow. I have Bunburyed all over Shropshire on two separate occasions. Now go on. Why are you Jack in the country and Ernest in town?

JACK My dear Algy, I don't know whether you will be able to understand my real motives. You are hardly serious enough. When one is placed in the position of a guardian, one has to adopt a very high moral tone, on all subjects. It is one's duty to do so, and as a high moral tone can hardly be said to conduce very much to either one's health or happiness if carried to excess, in order to get up to town I have always pretended I have a younger brother of the name of Ernest, who lives in the Albany and gets into the most dreadful scrapes. That, my dear Algy, is the whole truth, pure and simple.

ALGERNON The truth is rarely pure and never simple. Modern life would be very tedious if it was either. And modern literature a complete impossibility.

JACK That wouldn't be at all a bad thing.

ALGERNON Literary criticism is not your forte, my dear fellow. Don't try it. You should leave that to people who haven't been at a University. They do it so well in the daily papers. What you really are is a Bunburyist. I was quite right in saying you were a Bunburyist. You are one of the most advanced Bunburyists I know.

JACK What on earth do you mean?

ALGERNON You have invented a very useful younger brother called Ernest, in order that you may be able to come up to town as often as you like. I have invented an invaluable permanent invalid called Bunbury in order that I may go down into the country whenever I choose.

JACK What nonsense.

ALGERNON It isn't nonsense. Bunbury is perfectly invaluable. If it wasn't for Bunbury's extraordinary bad health for instance, I wouldn't be able to dine with you at the Savoy to-night, for I have been really engaged to Aunt Augusta for more than a week.

JACK I haven't asked you to dine with me anywhere to-night.

ALGERNON I know. You are absurdly careless about sending out invitations. It is very foolish of you. Nothing annoys people as much as not receiving invitations.

JACK Well, I can't dine at the Savoy. I owe them about £700. They are always getting judgments and things against me. They bother my life out.

ALGERNON Why on earth don't you pay them? You have got heaps of money.

JACK Yes, but Ernest hasn't, and I must keep up Ernest's reputation. Ernest is one of those chaps who never pay a bill. He gets writted about once a week.

ALGERNON Well, let us dine at Willis's.

JACK You had much better dine with your Aunt Augusta.

ALGERNON I haven't the smallest intention of doing anything of the kind. To begin with, I dined there on Monday, and once a week is quite enough to dine with one's own relations. In the second place, whenever I do dine there, I am always treated as a member of the family, and sent down with either no woman at all, or two. In the third place, I know perfectly well whom she will place me next to, to-night. She will place me next Mary Farquhar, who always flirts with her own husband across the dinner table. That is not very pleasant. Indeed, it is not even decent...and that sort of thing is enormously on the increase. The amount of women in London who flirt with their own husbands is perfectly scandalous. It looks so bad. It is simply washing one's clean linen in public. Besides, now that I know you to be a confirmed Bunburyist, I naturally want to talk to you about Bunburying. I want to tell you the rules.

JACK I am not a Bunburyist at all. If Gwendolen accepts me I shall naturally kill my brother. Indeed, I think I'll kill him in any case. Cecily is a good deal too much interested in him. She is always asking me to forgive him, and that sort of thing. It is rather a bore, so I am going to get rid of Ernest. And I strongly advise you to do the same with your friend Bunbury.

ALGERNON I haven't the smallest intention of doing anything of the kind, and if you ever get married, which seems to me extremely problematic, you will be very glad to know Bunbury. A man who marries without knowing Bunbury has a very tedious time of it.

JACK That is nonsense. If I marry a charming girl like Gwendolen, and she is the only girl I ever saw in my life that I would marry, I certainly won't want to know Bunbury,

ALGERNON Then your wife will. You don't seem to realise, my dear fellow, that in married life, three is company and two is none.

JACK (sententiously) That, my dear Algy, is the theory that the corrupt French drama has been propounding for the last fifty years.

ALGERNON Yes, and that the happy English home has proved in half the time. That is the worst of the English. They are always degrading truths into facts, and when a truth becomes a fact, it loses all its intellectual value.

JACK Do you always really understand what you say, Algy?

ALGERNON *(after consideration)* Yes...if I listen attentively.

A ring.

Ah! that must be Aunt Augusta! Now, if I get Aunt Augusta out of the way for ten minutes, so that you can have an opportunity for proposing to Gwendolen, may I dine with you to-night at Willis's?

JACK I suppose so, if you want to.

ALGERNON Yes, but you must be serious about it. I hate people who are not serious about meals. It is so shallow of them.

Enter LANE.

LANE Lady Bracknell and Miss Fairfax.

Enter LADY BRACKNELL *and* GWENDOLEN.

LADY BRACKNELL Well, dear Algernon, I hope you are well. *(Bows coldly to* JACK*)* Good afternoon, Mr Worthing.

ALGERNON *(going to meet them)* Good afternoon, Aunt Augusta. *(To* GWEN*)* Dear me, you are smart!

GWENDOLEN I am always smart.

ALGERNON I know: that is why I said it. If a woman isn't always smart, she is never smart.

GWENDOLEN Now don't try to be clever, Algy. It doesn't become you at all.

ALGERNON It is not becoming to anybody.

GWENDOLEN On the contrary. It is excessively becoming to me. *(To* JACK*)* Isn't it, Mr Worthing?

JACK Everything is becoming to you, Miss Fairfax.

LADY BRACKNELL Won't you come over and sit here, Gwendolen?

GWENDOLEN Thanks, mamma, I am quite comfortable where I am.

LADY BRACKNELL I am sorry if we are a little late, Algernon, but I was obliged to call on dear Lady Harbury. I hadn't been there since her poor husband's death. I never saw a woman so altered, she looks quite twenty years younger. I'll have a cup of tea now, and one of those nice cucumber sandwiches you promised me.

ALGERNON Certainly, Aunt Augusta. *(Goes over to table)* Good heavens! Why are there no cucumber sandwiches, Lane? I ordered them specially.

LANE *(gravely)* There were no cucumbers in the market this morning, sir. I went down twice.

ALGERNON No cucumbers!

LANE No, sir. Not even for ready money.

ALGERNON That will do, Lane, thank you.

LANE Thank you, sir.

Exit.

ALGERNON I am greatly distressed, Aunt Augusta, about there being no cucumbers, not even for ready money.

LADY BRACKNELL It makes no matter, Algernon, I had some crumpets with Lady Harbury, who seems to me to be living entirely for pleasure now.

ALGERNON Yes. I hear her hair has turned quite gold from grief.

LADY BRACKNELL It certainly has changed its colour. From what cause, of course, I can't say.

ALGERNON *hands tea.*

Thank you. I am going to send you down to dinner with Mary Farquhar, to-night. She is such a nice young woman and so attentive to her husband.

ALGERNON Do you know, I am afraid, Aunt Augusta, I shall have to give up the pleasure of dining with you to-night after all.

LADY BRACKNELL I hope not, Algernon.

ALGERNON Yes, it is a great bore, but the fact is I have just had a telegram to say that my poor friend Bunbury is very ill again. They seem to think I should be with him. I have promised to go down by the 6.40 from King's Gross.

LADY BRACKNELL It is very strange. This Mr Bunbury seems to suffer from curiously bad health.

ALGERNON Yes, dear old Bunbury is a terrible invalid.

LADY BRACKNELL Well, I must say, Algernon, that I think it is high time that Mr Bunbury made up his mind whether he was going to live or not. This shilly-shallying with the question is absurd. Nor do I in any way approve of this modern sympathy with invalids. I consider it morbid. Illness of any kind is hardly a thing to be encouraged in others. Health is the primary duty of life. I am always telling that to your poor uncle. But he never seems to take any notice... as far as any improvement in his many ailments goes. Well, Algernon, of course if you are obliged to be by the bedside of Mr Bunbury, I have nothing more to say. But I would be much obliged if you would ask Mr Bunbury from me to be kind enough not to have a relapse on Saturday, for I rely on you to arrange my music for me. It is my last reception, and one wants something that will encourage conversation— particularly at the end of the season, when everyone has practically said whatever they had to say.

ALGERNON Ah! That is the difficulty, Aunt Augusta. You see, if one plays good music people don't listen, and if one plays bad music they don't talk. But I'll tell you my ideas on the subject, if you will come into the next room for a moment. I have drawn out a programme.

LADY BRACKNELL Thank you, Algernon. It is very thoughtful of you. I'm sure the programme will be delightful, after a few expurgations. French songs I cannot possibly allow. People always seem to think that they are improper, and either look shocked, which is vulgar, or laugh, which is worse. But German sounds a thoroughly respectable language, and indeed, I believe is so. I will see you again, no doubt, Mr Worthing.

Exit **LADY BRACKNELL** *with* **ALGERNON**. **GWENDOLEN** *remains behind.*

JACK Charming day it has been, Miss Fairfax.

GWENDOLEN Pray don't talk to me about the weather, Mr Worthing: whenever people talk to me about the weather I always feel that they mean something else. And that makes me so nervous.

JACK I do mean something else.

GWENDOLEN I thought so. In fact, I am never wrong.

JACK And I would like to be allowed to take advantage of Lady Bracknell's temporary absence.

GWENDOLEN I would certainly advise you to do so. Mamma has a way of coming back suddenly into a room that I have often had to speak to her about.

JACK Miss Fairfax, ever since I met you I have admired you more than any girl I have ever met, since I met you.

GWENDOLEN Yes, I am quite aware of that. And I often wish that in public, at any rate, you had been more demonstrative. For me you have always had an irresistible fascination. Even before I met you I was far from indifferent to you.

JACK *looks at her in amazement.*

We live, as I hope you know, Mr Worthing, in an age of ideals. The fact is constantly mentioned in the more expensive monthly magazines, and has reached the provincial pulpits, I am told. And my ideal has always been to love someone of the name of Ernest. There is something in that name that inspires absolute confidence. The moment Algernon first mentioned to me that he had a friend called Ernest, I knew I was destined to love you. The name, fortunately for my peace of mind, is, as far as my own experience goes, extremely rare.

JACK You really love me, Gwendolen?

GWENDOLEN Passionately.

JACK Darling Gwendolen!

GWENDOLEN My own Ernest!

They embrace.

JACK Of course, you don't really mean to say that you couldn't love me if my name wasn't Ernest.

GWENDOLEN But your name is Ernest.

JACK Yes, I know it is. But supposing it was something else? Do you mean to say you couldn't love me then?

GWENDOLEN Ah, that is clearly a metaphysical speculation, and like all metaphysical speculations, has very little reference at all to the actual facts of real life, as we know them.

JACK Personally, darling, to speak quite candidly, I don't care much about the name of Ernest... I don't think the name suits me at all.

GWENDOLEN It suits you perfectly. It is a divine name. It has a music of its own. It produces vibrations.

JACK Well, really, Gwendolen, I must say that I think there are lots of other much nicer names. I think Jack, for instance, a charming name.

GWENDOLEN Jack? ...No, there is very little music in the name Jack, if any at all, indeed. It does not thrill. It produces absolutely no vibrations... I have known several Jacks, and they all without exception were more than usually plain. Besides, Jack is a notorious domesticity for John, and I pity any woman who is married to a man called John. She would have a very tedious life with him. She would probably never be allowed to know the pleasure of a single moment's solitude. The only really safe name is Ernest.

JACK Gwendolen, I must get christened at once—I mean we must get married at once. There is no time to be lost.

GWENDOLEN *(surprised)* Married, Mr Worthing?

JACK *(astounded)* Well...surely! You know that I love you, and you led me to believe, Miss Fairfax, that you were not absolutely indifferent to me.

GWENDOLEN I adore you. But you haven't proposed to me yet. Nothing has been said at all about marriage. The subject has not even been touched on.

JACK Well...may I propose to you now?

GWENDOLEN I think it would be an admirable opportunity. To spare you any possible disappointment, Mr Worthing, I think it only fair to tell you quite frankly beforehand that I am fully determined to accept you!

JACK Gwendolen!

GWENDOLEN Yes, Mr Worthing, what have you got to say to me?

JACK You know what I have got to say to you.

GWENDOLEN Yes, but you don't say it.

JACK Gwendolen, will you marry me? *(Goes on his knees)*

GWENDOLEN Of course I will, darling. How long you have been about it! I am afraid you have had very little experience in how to propose.

JACK My own one, I have never loved anyone in the world but you.

GWENDOLEN I know that. But men often propose for practice. I know my brother does. He tells me so... What wonderfully blue eyes you have, Ernest. They are quite, quite blue. I hope you will always look at me just like that, especially when there are other people present!

Enter **LADY BRACKNELL.**

LADY BRACKNELL Mr Worthing! Rise, sir, from this semi-recumbent posture. It is most indecorous.

JACK *rises.*

GWENDOLEN Mamma! I must beg you to retire. This is no place for you... Besides, Mr Worthing has not quite finished yet.

LADY BRACKNELL Finished what, may I ask?

GWENDOLEN I am engaged to Mr Worthing, mamma!

LADY BRACKNELL Pardon me, you are not engaged to anyone. When you do become engaged to someone, I or your father, should his health permit him, will inform you of the fact. An engagement should come on a young girl as a surprise, pleasant or unpleasant as the case may be. It is hardly a matter that she could be allowed to arrange for herself... And now, I have a few questions to put to you, Mr Worthing!

JACK I shall be charmed to reply to any questions, Lady Bracknell.

GWENDOLEN You mean if you know the answers to them. Mamma's questions are sometimes peculiarly inquisitorial.

LADY BRACKNELL I intend to make them very inquisitorial. And while I am making these enquiries, you, Gwendolen, will wait for me below in the carriage.

GWENDOLEN *(reproachfully)* Mamma!

LADY BRACKNELL *(severely)* In the carriage, Gwendolen.

GWENDOLEN *and* **JACK** *blow kisses to each other behind* **LADY BRACKNELL**'s *back.* **LADY BRACKNELL** *looks vaguely about as if she could not understand what the noise was. Finally turns round.*

Gwendolen! The carriage!

GWENDOLEN Yes, mamma!

Exit.

LADY BRACKNELL   *(sitting down)* You can take a chair, Mr Worthing. *(Looks in her pocket for note-book and pencil)*

JACK   Thank you, Lady Bracknell, I prefer standing.

LADY BRACKNELL   *(pencil and note-book in hand)* You are not down on my list of eligible young men, Mr Worthing, although I have the same list as the dear Duchess of Bolton has. We work together, in fact. However, I am quite ready to enter your name, should your answers be what a really affectionate mother requires. Do you smoke?

JACK   Well, yes, I must admit that I smoke.

LADY BRACKNELL   I am glad to hear it. A man should always have an occupation of some kind. There are far too many idle men in London as it is. How old are you?

JACK   Twenty-nine!

LADY BRACKNELL   A very good age to be married at. I have always been of opinion that a man who desires to get married should either know everything or nothing. Which do you know?

JACK   I know nothing, Lady Bracknell.

LADY BRACKNELL   I am pleased to hear it. I do not approve of anything that tampers with natural ignorance. Ignorance is like a delicate exotic fruit; touch it and the bloom is gone. What is your income?

JACK   Between seven and eight thousand a year.

LADY BRACKNELL   *(makes a note in her book)* In land, or in investments?

JACK   In investments, Lady Bracknell.

LADY BRACKNELL   That is satisfactory. What, between the duties expected of one during one's lifetime and the duties exacted from one after one's death—land has ceased to be either a profit or a pleasure. It gives one position and prevents one from keeping it up. That is all that can be said about it.

JACK I have a country house, with some land of course attached to it, but I don't depend on that for my real income. The poachers are the only people who make anything out of it.

LADY BRACKNELL A country house! How many bedrooms? Well, that point can be cleared up afterwards. *(Makes note)* You have a town house I hope. A girl with a simple unspoiled nature like Gwendolen could hardly be expected to reside in the country.

JACK Well, I own a house in Belgrave Square, but it is let by the year to Lady Bloxham. I have never lived in it. Of course, I can get it back whenever I like.

LADY BRACKNELL Lady Bloxham? I don't know her.

JACK Oh! she goes about very little. She is a lady considerably advanced in years.

LADY BRACKNELL Oh! nowadays that is no guarantee of respectability of character. What number in Belgrave Square?

JACK 149.

LADY BRACKNELL The unfashionable side. However, that could easily be altered.

JACK Do you mean the fashion or the side, Lady Bracknell?

LADY BRACKNELL Both if necessary, I presume. What are your politics?

JACK Well, I am afraid I really have none, Lady Bracknell. I am a Liberal Unionist.

LADY BRACKNELL Oh! they count as Tories! They dine with us. Or come in the evening, at any rate. You have, of course, no sympathy of any kind with the Radical Party?

JACK Oh! I don't want to put the asses against the classes, if that is what you mean, Lady Bracknell.

LADY BRACKNELL That is exactly what I do mean...ahem! ...Are your parents living?

JACK I have lost both my parents!

LADY BRACKNELL Both? ...To lose one parent may be regarded as a misfortune...to lose both seems like carelessness. Who was your father? Was he born in what the Radical papers call the purple of commerce or did he rise from the ranks of the aristocracy?

JACK I am afraid I don't really know. The fact is, Lady Bracknell, I said I had lost my parents. The truth is that my parents seem to have lost me... I don't actually know who I am. I was...well, I was found. The late Mr Thomas Cardew, an old gentleman of a very charitable and kindly disposition, found me and gave me the name of Worthing because he happened to have a ticket for Worthing in his pocket at the time. Worthing is a place in Sussex. It is a seaside resort.

LADY BRACKNELL Where did the charitable gentleman who had a ticket for the seaside resort find you?

JACK (gravely) In a handbag.

LADY BRACKNELL A handbag!

JACK (very seriously) Yes, Lady Bracknell. I was in a handbag—a somewhat large black leather handbag, with handles to it—an ordinary handbag, in fact.

LADY BRACKNELL In what locality did this Mr Cardew come across this ordinary handbag?

JACK In the cloak-room at Victoria Station. It was given to him in mistake for his own. He did not discover the error till he arrived at his own house. All subsequent efforts to ascertain who I was were unavailing.

LADY BRACKNELL The cloak-room at Victoria Station?

JACK Yes, the Brighton line.

LADY BRACKNELL The line is immaterial... Mr Worthing, I confess I feel somewhat bewildered by what you have just told me. To be born, or at any rate bred in a handbag, whether it had handles or not, seems to me to display a contempt for the ordinary decencies of family life that reminds one of the worst excesses of the French Revolution. And I presume you know what that unfortunate movement led to? As for the particular locality in which the handbag was found, a cloak-room at a railway station might serve to conceal a social indiscretion—has probably indeed been used for that purpose before now—but it could hardly be regarded as an assured basis for a recognised position in good society.

JACK May I ask then what you would advise me to do? I need hardly say I would do anything in the world to ensure Gwendolen's happiness.

LADY BRACKNELL I would strongly advise you, Mr Worthing, to try and acquire some relations as soon as possible, and to make a definite effort to produce, at any rate, one parent, of either sex, before the season is quite over.

JACK Well, I don't see how I could possibly manage to do that. I can produce the handbag at any moment. It is in my bedroom at home. I really think that should satisfy you, Lady Bracknell.

LADY BRACKNELL (*indignantly*) Me, sir? What has it to do with me? You can hardly imagine, sir, that I and Lord Bracknell would dream of allowing our only daughter—a girl brought up with the utmost care—to marry into a cloak-room and form an alliance with a parcel?

JACK *starts indignantly.*

Kindly open the door for me, sir. You will, of course, understand that for the future there is to be no communication of any kind between you and Miss Fairfax.

Exit.

ALGERNON, *from the other room, strikes up the* **"THE WEDDING MARCH"** , JACK *looks perfectly furious.*

JACK (*going to the door*) For goodness' sake don't play that ghastly tune, Algy. How idiotic you are!

Enter **ALGERNON** *cheerily.*

ALGERNON Didn't it go off all right, old boy? You don't mean to say Gwendolen refused you? If she did, you will have to propose again, that is all. If she refuses you a second time, she is sure to marry you.

JACK Oh, Gwendolen is as right as a trivet. As far as she is concerned, we are engaged. Her mother is perfectly unbearable. Never met such a Gorgon... I don't really know what a Gorgon is like, but I am quite sure that Lady Bracknell is one. Besides, she is a monster, without being a myth, which is rather unfair of her. I beg your pardon, Algy, I suppose I shouldn't talk about your own aunt in that way before you.

ALGERNON My dear boy, I love hearing my relatives abused. It is the only thing that makes me put up with them at all. Relations are simply a tedious pack of tedious people, who haven't got the remotest knowledge of how to live, nor the smallest instinct about when to die.

JACK Ah! I haven't got any relations. Don't know anything about relations.

ALGERNON You are a lucky fellow. Relations never lend one any money, and won't give one credit, even for genius. They are a sort of aggravated form of the public.

JACK And after all, what does it matter whether a man has ever had a father and mother or not? Mothers, of course, are all right. They pay a chap's bills and don't bother him. But fathers bother a chap and never pay his bills. I don't know a single chap at the club who speaks to his father.

ALGERNON Yes! Fathers are certainly not popular just at present. (*Takes up evening newspaper*)

JACK Popular! I bet you anything you like that there is not a single chap, of all the chaps that you and I know, who would be seen walking down St. James' Street with his own father. *(A pause)* Anything in the papers?

ALGERNON *(still reading)* Nothing.

JACK What a comfort.

ALGERNON There never is anything in the papers, as far as I can see.

JACK I think there is usually a great deal too much in them. They are always bothering one about people one doesn't know, one has never met, and one doesn't care twopence about. Brutes!

ALGERNON I think people one hasn't met are charming. I'm very much interested at present in a girl I have never met; very much interested indeed.

JACK Oh! that is nonsense.

ALGERNON It isn't.

JACK Well, I won't argue about the matter. You always want to argue about things.

ALGERNON That is exactly what things were originally made for.

JACK Upon my word, if I thought that, I'd shoot myself... *(A pause)* You don't think there is any chance of Gwendolen becoming like her mother in about a hundred and fifty years, do you, Algy?

ALGERNON *(drawling and sententiously)* All women become like their mothers. That is their tragedy. No man does. That is his.

JACK Is that clever?

ALGERNON It is perfectly phrased and quite as true as anything in modern life should be.

JACK I am sick to death of cleverness. Everybody is clever nowadays. You can't go anywhere without meeting clever people. The thing has become an absolute public nuisance. I wish to goodness we had a few fools left.

ALGERNON We have.

JACK Well, I should extremely like to meet them. What do they talk about?

ALGERNON The fools? Oh! about the clever people, of course.

JACK What fools! ...

ALGERNON By the way, did you tell Gwendolen the truth about your being Ernest in town and Jack in the country?

JACK (*in a very patronising manner*) My dear fellow, the truth isn't quite the sort of thing one tells to a nice, sweet, refined girl. What extraordinary ideas you have about the way to behave to women!

ALGERNON The only way to behave to women is to make love to them if they are pretty, and to someone else if they are plain.

JACK Oh! that is nonsense!

ALGERNON What about the young lady whose guardian you are! Miss Cardew?

JACK Oh! Cecily is all right. Before the end of the week I shall have got rid of my brother... I think I'll probably kill him in Paris.

ALGERNON Why Paris?

JACK Oh! less trouble: no nonsense about a funeral and that sort of thing—yes, I'll kill him in Paris... Apoplexy will do perfectly well. Lots of people die of apoplexy, quite suddenly, don't they?

ALGERNON Yes, but it's hereditary, my dear fellow. It's a sort of thing that runs in families.

JACK Good heavens! Then I certainly won't choose that. What can I say?

ALGERNON Oh! say the influenza.

JACK Oh, no! that wouldn't sound probable at all. Far too many people have had it.

ALGERNON Oh well! Say anything you choose. Say a severe chill. That's all right.

JACK You are sure a severe chill isn't hereditary, or anything dreadful of that kind?

ALGERNON Of course it isn't.

JACK Very well then. That is settled.

ALGERNON But I thought you said that Miss Cardew was a little too much interested in your poor brother Ernest?

JACK Oh! that is all right. Cecily is not a romantic girl at all. She has got a capital appetite, and goes on long walks, and everything of that kind.

ALGERNON I should rather like to see Cecily.

JACK I will take very good care you never do. And you are not to speak of her as Cecily.

ALGERNON Ah! I believe she is plain. Yes: I know perfectly well what she is like. She is one of those dull, intellectual girls, one meets all over the place. Girls who have got large minds and large feet. I am sure she is more than usually plain, and I suspect she is about thirty-nine, and looks it.

JACK She happens to be excessively pretty, and she is only just eighteen.

ALGERNON Have you told Gwendolen yet that you have an excessively pretty ward who is only just eighteen?

JACK Oh! one doesn't blurt these things out to people. Life is a question of tact. One leads up to the thing gradually. Cecily and Gwendolen are perfectly certain to be extremely great friends. Probably half an hour after they have met, they will be calling each other sister.

ALGERNON Women only do that when they have had a fearful quarrel and called each other a lot of other things first... Now, my dear boy, if we want to get a good table at Willis's, we really must go and dress. Do you know it is nearly seven?

JACK Oh! it always is nearly seven!

ALGERNON Well, I'm hungry.

JACK I never knew you when you weren't... However, all right. I'll go round to the Albany and meet you at Willis's at eight. You can call for me on your way, if you like.

ALGERNON Very well. And what shall we do after dinner? Go to a theatre?

JACK Oh no! I loathe listening.

ALGERNON Well, let us go to the Club.

JACK No! I hate talking.

ALGERNON Well, we might trot round to the Empire at ten?

JACK Oh no! I can't bear looking at things. It is so silly.

ALGERNON Well, what shall we do?

JACK Oh, nothing!

ALGERNON It is awfully hard work doing nothing. However, I don't mind hard work when there is no definite object of any kind...

Enter LANE.

LANE Miss Fairfax.

Enter GWENDOLEN.

Exit LANE.

ALGERNON Gwendolen!

GWENDOLEN Algy, kindly turn your back. I have something very particular to say to Mr Worthing. As it is somewhat of a private matter, you will of course listen.

ALGERNON Really, Gwendolen, I don't think I can allow this at all.

GWENDOLEN Algy, you always adopt a strictly immoral attitude towards life. You are not quite old enough to do that. Pray oblige me by looking out of the window.

ALGERNON *turns away.*

Ernest!

JACK My own darling!

GWENDOLEN We may never be married, Ernest. From the expression on mamma's face, I fear we never shall. Few parents nowadays pay any regard to what their children say to them! The old-fashioned respect for the young is rapidly dying out. Whatever influence I ever had over mamma I lost at the age of two. But though she may prevent us from becoming man and wife, and I may marry someone else— and marry often, nothing that she can possibly do can alter my eternal devotion to you.

JACK Dear Gwendolen!

GWENDOLEN The story of your romantic origin, as related to me by mamma, with unpleasing comments, has naturally stirred the deeper fibres of my nature. Your Christian name is an irresistible fascination. The simplicity of your nature makes you exquisitely incomprehensible to me. Your town address at the Albany I have. What is your address in the country?

JACK The Manor House, Woolton, Hertfordshire.

ALGERNON *writes the address on his cuff.*

GWENDOLEN There is a good postal service, I suppose? It may be necessary to do something desperate. That, of course, will require serious consideration. I will communicate with you daily.

JACK My own one.

GWENDOLEN Algy, you may turn round now. Good-bye.

Exit GWENDOLEN.

JACK What a splendid creature! The only girl I have ever loved in my life. Now let us go off and dine—I'll give you the best dinner in London. What on earth are you laughing at?

ALGERNON I hope to goodness to-morrow will be a fine day.

JACK It never is...but what are you going to do tomorrow?

ALGERNON To-morrow, my dear boy, I am going Bunburying.

JACK What nonsense!

ALGERNON I love nonsense.

Act drop.

ACT II

SCENE: Garden at the Manor House. Door leading into house right. The garden is an old-fashioned one full of roses and yew-hedges. Time of year, July. Basket chairs and a table covered with books.

MISS PRISM *discovered seated at the table.*

MISS PRISM *(calling)* Cecily, Cecily! Surely such a utilitarian occupation as the watering of flowers is rather Moulton's duty than yours? Especially at a moment when intellectual pleasures await you. Your German lesson has been waiting for you for nearly twenty minutes.

Enter CECILY *with a watering-pot.*

CECILY Oh! I wish you would give Moulton the German lesson instead of me. Moulton!

MOULTON *(looking out from behind a hedge, with a broad grin on his face)* Eh, Miss Cecily?

CECILY Wouldn't you like to know German, Moulton? German is the language talked by people who live in Germany.

MOULTON *(shaking his head)* I don't hold with them furrin tongues, miss. *(Bowing to* MISS PRISM*)* No offence to you, ma'am. *(Disappears behind hedge)*

MISS PRISM Cecily, this will never do. Pray open your Schiller at once.

CECILY But I don't like German. It isn't at all a becoming language. I know perfectly well that I look quite plain after my German lesson.

MISS PRISM Child, you know how anxious your guardian is that you should improve yourself in every way. He laid particular stress on your German, as he was leaving for town yesterday.

CECILY Dear Uncle Jack is so very serious! Sometimes he is so serious that I think he cannot be quite well.

MISS PRISM Your guardian enjoys the best of health, and his gravity of demeanour is especially to be commended in one so comparatively young as he is. I know no one who has a higher sense of duty and responsibility.

CECILY I suppose that is why he often looks a little bored when we three are together.

MISS PRISM Cecily! I am surprised at you. Mr Worthing has many troubles in his life. Idle merriment and triviality would be out of place in his conversation. You must remember his constant anxiety about that unfortunate young man his brother.

CECILY I wish Uncle Jack would allow that unfortunate young man, his brother, to come down here sometimes. We might have a good influence over him, Miss Prism. I am sure you certainly would. You know German, and geology, and things of that kind that influence a man very much. (CECILY *begins to write in her diary*)

MISS PRISM (*shaking her head*) I do not think that even I could produce any effect on a character that according to his own brother's admission is irretrievably weak and vacillating. Indeed, I am not sure that I would desire to reclaim him. I am not in favour of this modern mania for turning bad people into good people at a moment's notice. As a man sows so let him reap.

CECILY But men don't sew, Miss Prism... And if they did, I don't see why they should be punished for it. There is a great deal too much punishment in the world. German is a punishment, certainly, and there is far too much German. You told me yourself yesterday that Germany was over-populated.

MISS PRISM That is no reason why you should be writing your diary instead of translating "William Tell". You must put away your diary, Cecily. I really don't see why you should keep a diary at all.

CECILY I keep a diary in order to enter the wonderful secrets of my life. If I didn't write them down, I should probably forget all about them.

MISS PRISM Memory, my dear Cecily, is the diary that we all carry about with us.

CECILY Yes, but it usually chronicles the things that have never happened, and couldn't possibly have happened. I believe that Memory is responsible for nearly all the three-volume novels that every cultivated woman writes nowadays and no educated man ever reads.

MISS PRISM Do not speak slightingly of the three-volume novel, Cecily. I wrote one myself in earlier days.

CECILY Did you really, Miss Prism? How wonderfully clever you are! I hope it did not end happily? I don't like novels that end happily. They depress me so much.

MISS PRISM The good ended happily, and the bad unhappily. That is what Fiction means.

CECILY I suppose so. But it seems very unfair. And was your novel ever published?

MISS PRISM Alas! no. The manuscript unfortunately was abandoned. I use the word in the sense of lost or mislaid. To your work, child, these speculations are profitless.

CECILY (smiling) But I see dear Dr Chasuble coming up through the garden.

MISS PRISM (rising and advancing) Dr Chasuble! This is indeed a pleasure.

Enter canon CHASUBLE.

DR CHASUBLE And how are we this morning? Miss Prism, you are, I trust, well?

CECILY Miss Prism has just been complaining of a slight headache. I think it would do her so much good to have a short stroll with you in the Park, Dr Chasuble.

MISS PRISM Cecily, I have not mentioned anything about a headache.

CECILY No, dear Miss Prism, I know that, but I felt instinctively that you had a headache. Indeed, I was thinking about that, and not about my German lesson, when the Rector came in.

DR CHASUBLE I hope, Cecily, you are not inattentive.

CECILY Oh, I am afraid I am terribly inattentive.

DR CHASUBLE That is strange. Were I fortunate enough to be Miss Prism's pupil, I would hang upon her lips, *(***MISS PRISM** *glares)* I spoke metaphorically...metaphorically. *(Walks across stage)* My metaphor was drawn from bees. Ahem! Mr Worthing, I suppose, has not returned from town yet?

MISS PRISM We do not expect him till Monday afternoon.

DR CHASUBLE Ah yes, he usually likes to spend his Sunday in London. He is not one of those whose sole aim is enjoyment, as, by all accounts, that unfortunate young man his brother seems to be. But I must not disturb Egeria and her pupil any longer.

MISS PRISM Egeria? My name is Laetitia, Doctor.

DR CHASUBLE *(bowing)* A classical allusion merely, drawn from the Pagan authors. I shall see you both no doubt at Evensong?

MISS PRISM I think, dear Doctor, I will have a stroll with you. It might do my headache good.

DR CHASUBLE With pleasure, Miss Prism, with pleasure. We might go as far as the schools and back.

MISS PRISM That would be delightful. Cecily, you will read your Political Economy in my absence. The chapter on the Fall of the Rupee you may omit. It is somewhat too sensational for a young girl. Even these metallic problems have their melodramatic side.

DR CHASUBLE Reading Political Economy, Cecily? It is wonderful how girls are educated nowadays. I suppose you know all about the relations between Capital and Labour?

CECILY I am afraid I am not learned at all. All I know is about the relations between Capital and Idleness—and that is merely from observation. So I don't suppose it is true.

MISS PRISM Cecily, that sounds like Socialism! And I suppose you know where Socialism leads to?

CECILY Oh, yes! That leads to Rational Dress, Miss Prism. And I suppose that when a woman is dressed rationally, she is treated rationally. She certainly deserves to be.

DR CHASUBLE A wilful lamb! Dear child!

MISS PRISM *(smiling)* A sad trouble sometimes.

DR CHASUBLE I envy you such tribulation.

Exit with **MISS PRISM**.

CECILY *(throws all the books on the ground)* Horrid Political Economy! Horrid Geography! Horrid, horrid German!

Enter **MERRIMAN** *with a card on a salver.*

MERRIMAN Mr Ernest Worthing has just driven over from the station. He has brought his luggage with him.

CECILY *(takes the card and reads it)* "Mr Ernest Worthing, B.4, The Albany, W." Uncle Jack's brother! Did you tell him Mr Worthing was in town?

MERRIMAN Yes, Miss. He seemed very much disappointed. I mentioned that you and Miss Prism were in the garden. He said he was anxious to speak to you both for a moment.

CECILY *(to herself)* I don't think Miss Prism would like my being alone with him. So I had better send for him at once, before she comes in. *(To* **MERRIMAN***)* Ask Mr Ernest

Worthing to come here. I suppose you had better speak to the housekeeper about a room for him.

MERRIMAN I have already sent his luggage up to the Blue Room, miss: next to Mr Worthing's own room.

CECILY Oh! that is all right.

Exit MERRIMAN.

I have never met any really wicked person before. I feel rather frightened. I am so afraid he will look just like everyone else.

Enter ALGERNON, *very gay and debonair.*

He does!

ALGERNON *(raising his hat)* You are little Miss Cecily, I am sure.

CECILY You are under some strange mistake. I am not little. In fact, I believe I am more than usually tall for my age. (ALGERNON *is rather taken aback*). You, I see from your card, are Uncle Jack's wicked brother.

ALGERNON I am not really wicked at all, Miss Cecily. You mustn't think that I am wicked.

CECILY If you are not, then you have certainly been deceiving us all in a very inexcusable manner. You have made Uncle Jack believe that you are very bad. I hope you have not been leading a double life, pretending to be wicked and being really good all the time. That would be hypocrisy.

ALGERNON *(looks at her in amazement)* Oh! of course I have been rather reckless.

CECILY I am glad to hear it.

ALGERNON In fact, I have been very wicked in my own small way.

CECILY I don't think you should look so pleased, though I am sure it must have been very pleasant.

ALGERNON It is much pleasanter being here with you.

CECILY I can't understand how you are here at all. Uncle Jack telegraphed to you yesterday at the Albany that he would see you for the last time at six o'clock. He lets me read all the telegrams he sends you. I know some of them by heart.

ALGERNON The fact is I didn't get the telegram till it was too late. Then I missed him at the Club, and the Hall Porter said he thought he had come down here. So, of course, I followed as I knew he wanted to see me.

CECILY He won't be back till Monday afternoon.

ALGERNON That is a great disappointment. I am obliged to go up by the first train on Monday morning. I have a business appointment that I am anxious...to miss!

CECILY Couldn't you miss it anywhere but in London?

ALGERNON No: the appointment is in London.

CECILY Well, I know, of course, how important it is not to keep a business engagement, if one wants to retain any sense of the beauty of life, but still I think you had better wait till Uncle Jack arrives. I know he wants to speak to you about your emigrating.

ALGERNON About my what?

CECILY Your emigrating. He has gone up to buy your outfit.

ALGERNON I certainly wouldn't let Jack buy my outfit. He has no taste in neckties at all.

CECILY I don't think you will require neckties. Uncle Jack is sending you to Australia.

ALGERNON Australia! I'd sooner shoot myself.

CECILY Well, he said on Wednesday night, that you would have to choose between this world, the next world, and Australia.

ALGERNON Oh, well! The accounts I have received of Australia and the next world are not particularly encouraging. This world is good enough for me, cousin Cecily.

CECILY Yes, but are you good enough for it?

ALGERNON I wish you would reform me. You might make that your mission.

CECILY How dare you suggest that I have a mission?

ALGERNON I beg your pardon: but I thought every woman had a mission of some kind, nowadays.

CECILY Every female has! No woman. Besides, I have no time to reform you this afternoon.

ALGERNON Well, would you mind my reforming myself this afternoon?

CECILY It is rather Quixotic of you. But I think you should try.

ALGERNON I feel better already.

CECILY You are looking a little worse.

ALGERNON That is because I am hungry.

CECILY How thoughtless of me. I should have remembered that when one is going to lead an entirely new life, one requires regular and wholesome meals. Miss Prism and I lunch at two, off some roast mutton.

ALGERNON I fear that would be too rich for me.

CECILY Uncle Jack, whose health has been sadly undermined by the late hours you keep in town, has been ordered by his London doctor to have pâté de foie gras sandwiches and 1874 champagne at twelve. I don't know if such invalid fare would suit you.

ALGERNON Oh! I will be quite content with '74 champagne.

CECILY I am glad to see you have such simple tastes. This is the dining-room.

ALGERNON Thank you. Might I have a buttonhole first? I have never any appetite unless I have a buttonhole first.

CECILY A Maréchal Niel?

ALGERNON No, I'd sooner have a pink rose.

CECILY Why?

ALGERNON Because you are just like a pink rose, Miss Cecily.

CECILY I don't think it can be right for you to talk to me like that. Miss Prism never says such things to me.

ALGERNON Then Miss Prism is a short-sighted old lady. *(CECILY puts the rose in his buttonhole)* You are the prettiest girl I ever saw.

CECILY Miss Prism says that all good looks are a snare.

ALGERNON They are a snare that every sensible man would like to be caught in.

CECILY Oh, I don't think I would care to catch a sensible man. I wouldn't know what to talk to him about.

They pass into the house. MISS PRISM *and* DR CHASUBLE *return.*

MISS PRISM You are too much alone, dear Dr Chasuble. You should get married. A misanthrope I can understand—a womanthrope, never!

DR CHASUBLE *(with a scholar's shudder)* Believe me, I do not deserve so neologistic a phrase. The precept as well as the practice of the Primitive Church was distinctly against matrimony.

MISS PRISM *(sententiously)* That is obviously the reason why the Primitive Church has not lasted up to the present day. And you do not seem to realise, dear Doctor, that by persistently remaining single, a man converts himself into a permanent public temptation. You should be more careful; you may lead weaker vessels astray.

DR CHASUBLE But is a man not equally attractive when married?

MISS PRISM No married man is ever attractive except to his wife.

DR CHASUBLE And often, I've been told, not even to her.

MISS PRISM That depends on the intellectual sympathies of the woman. Maturity can always be depended on. Ripeness can be trusted. Young women are green, *(DR CHASUBLE starts)* I spoke horticulturally. My metaphor was drawn from fruits.

Enter JACK *slowly from the back of the garden. He is dressed in the deepest mourning, with crape hatband and black gloves.*

Mr Worthing! This is indeed a surprise. We did not look for you till Monday afternoon.

JACK *(shakes* MISS PRISM*'s hand in a tragic manner)* I have returned sooner than I expected. Dr Chasuble, I hope you are well?

DR CHASUBLE Dear Mr Worthing, I trust this garb of woe does not betoken some terrible calamity?

JACK *(sitting down)* My brother.

MISS PRISM More shameful debts and extravagances?

DR CHASUBLE Still leading his life of pleasure?

JACK *(shaking his head)* Dead!

DR CHASUBLE Your brother Ernest dead?

JACK Quite dead.

MISS PRISM What a lesson for him! I trust he will profit by it.

DR CHASUBLE Death is the inheritance of us all, Miss Prism. Nor should we look on it as a special judgment, but rather as a general providence. Life were incomplete without it... Mr Worthing, I offer you my sincere condolence. You have at least the consolation of knowing that you were always the most generous and forgiving of brothers.

JACK Poor Ernest! He had many faults, but it is a sad blow.

DR CHASUBLE Very sad indeed... Were you with him at the end?

JACK No. He died abroad, in Paris. I had a telegram last night from the manager of the Hotel.

DR CHASUBLE Was the cause of death mentioned?

JACK A severe chill, it seems.

MISS PRISM As a man sows, so shall he reap.

DR CHASUBLE *(raising his hand)* Charity, dear Miss Prism, charity! None of us are perfect. I myself am peculiarly susceptible to draughts. Will the...interment take place here?

JACK No. He seems to have expressed a desire to be buried in Paris.

DR CHASUBLE In Paris? *(Shakes his head)* I fear that hardly points to any very serious state of mind at the last. You would no doubt wish me to make some slight allusion to this tragic domestic affliction next Sunday. (**JACK** *presses his hand convulsively)* My sermon on the meaning of the manna in the wilderness can be adapted to almost any occasion, joyful, or, as in the present case, distressing. I have preached it at harvest celebrations, christenings, confirmations, on days of humiliation and festal days. The last time I delivered it was in the Cathedral, as a charity sermon on behalf of the Society for the Prevention of Discontent among the Upper Orders. The Bishop, who was present, was much struck by some of the analogies I drew.

JACK Ah! that reminds me, you mentioned christenings, I think, Dr Chasuble? I suppose you know how to christen all right? (**DR CHASUBLE** *looks astounded)* I mean, of course, you are continually christening, aren't you?

MISS PRISM It is, I regret to say, one of the Rector's most constant duties in this parish. I have often spoken to the poorer classes about it.

DR CHASUBLE The Church rejects no babe, Miss Prism. In every child, there is the making of a saint. But is there any particular infant in whom you are interested, Mr Worthing? Your brother was, I believe, unmarried, was he not?

JACK *(mournfully)* Oh! yes.

MISS PRISM *(bitterly)* People who live entirely for pleasure usually are.

JACK But it is not for any child, dear Doctor. I am very fond of children. No! the fact is, I would like to be christened myself, this afternoon, if you have nothing better to do.

DR CHASUBLE But surely, Mr Worthing, you have been christened already?

JACK I don't remember anything about it.

DR CHASUBLE But have you any grave doubts on the subject?

JACK I have the very gravest doubts. There are circumstances, unnecessary to mention at present, connected with my birth and early life that make me think I was a good deal neglected. I certainly wasn't properly looked after, at any rate. Of course I don't know if the thing would bother you in any way, or if you think I am a little too old now.

DR CHASUBLE Oh! I am not by any means a bigoted Paedo-baptist. The sprinkling and, indeed, the immersion of adults was a common practice of the Primitive Church.

JACK Immersion! You don't mean to say that...

DR CHASUBLE You need have no apprehensions. Sprinkling is all that is necessary, or indeed I think advisable. Our weather is so changeable. At what hour would you wish the ceremony performed?

JACK Oh! I might trot round after lunch, about three, if that would suit you.

DR CHASUBLE Oh! perfectly. In fact I have two similar ceremonies to perform at that time. A case of twins that occurred recently in one of the outlying cottages on your own estate. Poor Jenkins the carter, a most hard-working man.

JACK Oh! I don't see much fun in being christened along with other babies. It would be childish. Would half past five do?

DR CHASUBLE Admirably! Admirably! (*Enters note*) And now, dear Mr Worthing, I will not intrude any longer into a house of sorrow. I would merely beg you not to be too much bowed down by grief. What seem to us bitter trials are often blessings in disguise.

MISS PRISM This seems to me a blessing of an extremely obvious kind.

Enter CECILY *from the house.*

CECILY Uncle Jack! Oh, I am pleased to see you back. *(Goes towards him. He kisses her brow in a melancholy manner)* What horrid clothes you have got on! Do go and change them.

MISS PRISM Cecily!

CECILY What is the matter? Uncle Jack, do look happy! You look as if you had toothache, and I have got such a surprise for you. Who do you think is in the dining-room? Your brother!

JACK Who?

CECILY Your brother Ernest. He arrived about half an hour ago.

JACK What nonsense! I haven't got a brother.

CECILY Oh, don't say that. However badly he may have behaved to you in the past he is still your brother. You couldn't be so heartless as to disown him. I'll tell him to come out. And you will shake hands with him, won't you, Uncle Jack?

Exit.

DR CHASUBLE These are very joyful tidings. That telegram from Paris seems to have been a somewhat heartless jest by one who wished to play upon your feelings.

MISS PRISM After we had all been resigned to his loss, his sudden return seems to me peculiarly distressing.

JACK My brother is in the dining-room? I don't know what it all means. I think it is perfectly absurd.

Enter ALGERNON *and* CECILY.

ALGERNON *(going right over to* JACK *and holding out his hand)* Brother John, I have come down from town to tell you that I am very sorry for all the trouble I have given you, and that I intend to lead a better life in the future. *(*JACK *glares at him and does not take his hand)*

DR CHASUBLE *(to* **MISS PRISM***)* There is good in that young man. He seems to be sincerely repentant.

MISS PRISM These sudden conversions do not please me. They belong to Dissent. They savour of the laxity of the Nonconformist.

CECILY Uncle Jack, you are not going to refuse your own brother's hand?

JACK Nothing will induce me to take his hand. I think his coming down here disgraceful. He knows perfectly well why.

DR CHASUBLE Young man, you have had a very narrow escape of your life. I hope it will be a warning to you. We were mourning your demise when you entered.

ALGERNON Yes, I see Jack has got a new suit of clothes. They don't fit him properly. His necktie is wrong.

CECILY Uncle Jack, do be nice. There is some good in everyone. Ernest has just been telling me about his poor invalid friend Mr Bunbury whom he goes to visit so often. If a young man leaves London to go and see a sick friend, there must be some good in him.

JACK Oh! he has been talking about Bunbury, has he?

CECILY Yes, he has told me all about poor Mr Bunbury, and his terrible state of health.

JACK Bunbury! Well, I won't have him talk to you about Bunbury or about anything else. It is enough to drive one perfectly frantic.

DR CHASUBLE Mr Worthing, your brother has been unexpectedly restored to you by the mysterious dispensations of providence, who seems to desire your reconciliation. And indeed it is good for brothers to dwell together in amity.

ALGERNON Of course I admit that the faults were all on my side. But I must say that I think that Brother John's coldness to me is peculiarly painful. I expected a warmer welcome, especially considering it is the first time I have come here.

CECILY Uncle Jack! Do shake hands with Ernest. I will never forgive you, if you don't.

JACK Never forgive me?

CECILY Never, never, never!

JACK I suppose I must, then. *(Shakes hands)* You young scoundrel! You must get out of this place as soon as possible. I don't allow any Bunburying here.

Enter MERRIMAN.

MERRIMAN I have put Mr Ernest's things in the room next to yours, sir. I suppose that is all right?

JACK What?

MERRIMAN Mr Ernest's luggage, sir. I have unpacked it and put it in the room next to your own.

JACK His luggage?

MERRIMAN Yes, sir. Three portmanteaus, a dressing-case, two hat-boxes, and a large luncheon-basket.

ALGERNON I am afraid I can't stay more than a week this time.

MERRIMAN *(to* ALGERNON*)* I beg your pardon, sir, there is an elderly gentleman wishes to see you. He has just come in a cab from the station. *(Hands card on salver)*

ALGERNON To see me?

MERRIMAN Yes, sir.

ALGERNON *(reads card)* Parker and Gribsby, Solicitors. I don't know anything about them. Who are they?

JACK *(takes card)* Parker and Gribsby. I wonder who they can be. I expect, Ernest, they have come about some business for your friend Bunbury. Perhaps Bunbury wants to make his will and wishes you to be executor. *(To* MERRIMAN*)* Show the gentleman in at once.

MERRIMAN Very good, sir.

Exit.

JACK I hope, Ernest, that I may rely on the statement you made to me last week when I finally settled all your bills for you. I hope you have no outstanding accounts of any kind.

ALGERNON I haven't any debts at all, dear Jack. Thanks to your generosity I don't owe a penny, except for a few neckties, I believe.

JACK I am sincerely glad to hear it.

Enter **MERRIMAN**.

MERRIMAN Mr Gribsby.

Exit.

Enter **GRIBSBY**.

GRIBSBY *(to* **DR CHASUBLE***)* Mr Ernest Worthing?

MISS PRISM This is Mr Ernest Worthing.

GRIBSBY Mr Ernest Worthing?

ALGERNON Yes.

GRIBSBY Of B.4, The Albany?

ALGERNON Yes, that is my address.

GRIBSBY I am very sorry, sir, but we have a writ of attachment for twenty days against you at the suit of the Savoy Hotel Co. Limited for £762 14s. 2d.

ALGERNON Against me?

GRIBSBY Yes, sir.

ALGERNON What perfect nonsense! I never dine at the Savoy at my own expense. I always dine at Willis's. It is far more expensive. I don't owe a penny to the Savoy.

GRIBSBY The writ is marked as having been served on you personally at The Albany on May the 27th. Judgment was given in default against you on the fifth of June. Since then we have written to you no less than fifteen times, without receiving any reply. In the interest of our clients we had no option but to obtain an order for committal of your person.

ALGERNON Committal! What on earth do you mean by committal? I haven't the smallest intention of going away. I am staying here for a week. I am staying with my brother. If you imagine I am going up to town the moment I arrive you are extremely mistaken.

GRIBSBY I am merely a Solicitor myself. I do not employ personal violence of any kind. The Officer of the Court, whose function it is to seize the person of the debtor, is waiting in the fly outside. He has considerable experience in these matters. That is why we always employ him. But no doubt you will prefer to pay the bill.

ALGERNON Pay it? How on earth am I going to do that? You don't suppose I have got any money? How perfectly silly you are. No gentleman ever has any money.

GRIBSBY My experience is that it is usually relations who pay.

ALGERNON Jack, you really must settle this bill.

JACK Kindly allow me to see the particular items, Mr Gribsby... *(Turns over immense folio)* ...£762 14*s*. 2*d*. since last October. I am bound to say I never saw such reckless extravagance in all my life. *(Hands it to* **DR CHASUBLE***)*

MISS PRISM £762 for eating! There can be little good in any young man who eats so much, and so often.

DR CHASUBLE We are far away from Wordsworth's plain living and high thinking.

JACK Now, Dr Chasuble, do you consider that I am in any way called upon to pay this monstrous account for my brother?

DR CHASUBLE I am bound to say that I do not think so. It would be encouraging his profligacy.

MISS PRISM As a man sows, so let him reap. This proposed incarceration might be most salutary. It is to be regretted that it is only for twenty days.

JACK I am quite of your opinion.

ALGERNON My dear fellow, how ridiculous you are! You know perfectly well that the bill is really yours.

JACK Mine?

ALGERNON Yes, you know it is.

DR CHASUBLE Mr Worthing, if this is a jest, it is out of place.

MISS PRISM It is gross effrontery. Just what I expected from him.

CECILY And it is ingratitude. I didn't expect that.

JACK Never mind what he says. This is the way he always goes on. You mean now to say that you are not Ernest Worthing, residing at B.4, The Albany. I wonder, as you are at it, that you don't deny being my brother at all. Why don't you?

ALGERNON Oh! I am not going to do that, my dear fellow. It would be absurd. Of course I'm your brother. And that is why you should pay this bill for me.

JACK I will tell you quite candidly that I have not the smallest intention of doing anything of the kind. Dr Chasuble, the worthy Rector of this parish, and Miss Prism, in whose admirable and sound judgment I place great reliance, are both of the opinion that incarceration would do you a great deal of good. And I think so, too.

GRIBSBY *(pulls out watch)* I am sorry to disturb this pleasant family meeting, but time presses. We have to be at Holloway not later than four o'clock; otherwise it is difficult to obtain admission. The rules are very strict.

ALGERNON Holloway!

GRIBSBY It is at Holloway that detentions of this character take place always.

ALGERNON Well, I really am not going to be imprisoned in the suburbs for having dined in the West End.

GRIBSBY The bill is for suppers, not for dinners.

ALGERNON I really don't care. All I say is that I am not going to be imprisoned in the suburbs.

GRIBSBY The surroundings I admit are middle class; but the gaol itself is fashionable and well-aired; and there are ample opportunities of taking exercise at certain stated hours of the day. In the case of a medical certificate, which is always easy to obtain, the hours can be extended.

ALGERNON Exercise! Good God! No gentleman ever takes exercise. You don't seem to understand what a gentleman is.

GRIBSBY I have met so many of them, sir, that I am afraid I don't. There are the most curious varieties of them. The result of cultivation, no doubt. Will you kindly come now, sir, if it will not be inconvenient to you.

ALGERNON (appealingly) Jack!

MISS PRISM Pray be firm, Mr Worthing.

DR CHASUBLE This is an occasion on which any weakness would be out of place. It would be a form of self-deception.

JACK I am quite firm, and I don't know what weakness or deception of any kind is.

CECILY Uncle Jack! I think you have a little money of mine, haven't you? Let me pay this bill. I wouldn't like your own brother to be in prison.

JACK Oh! I couldn't possibly let you pay it, Cecily. That would be absurd.

CECILY Then you will, won't you? I think you would be sorry if you thought your own brother was shut up. Of course, I am quite disappointed with him.

JACK You won't speak to him again, Cecily, will you?

CECILY Certainly not, unless, of course, he speaks to me first. It would be very rude not to answer him.

JACK Well, I'll take care he doesn't speak to you. I'll take care he doesn't speak to anybody in this house. The man should be cut. Mr Gribsby...

GRIBSBY Yes, sir.

JACK I'll pay this bill for my brother. It is the last bill I shall ever pay for him, too. How much is it?

GRIBSBY £762 14*s.* 2*d.* Ah! The cab will be five-and-nine-pence extra: hired for the convenience of the client.

JACK All right.

MISS PRISM I must say that I think such generosity quite foolish.

DR CHASUBLE *(with a wave of the hand)* The heart has its wisdom as well as the head, Miss Prism.

JACK Payable to Parker and Gribsby, I suppose?

GRIBSBY Yes, sir. Kindly don't cross the cheque. Thank you. *(To* DR CHASUBLE*)* Good day. *(*DR CHASUBLE *bows coldly)* Good day. *(*MISS PRISM *bows coldly) (To* ALGERNON*)* I hope I shall have the pleasure of meeting you again.

ALGERNON I sincerely hope not. What ideas you have of the sort of society a gentleman wants to mix in. No gentleman ever wants to know a Solicitor who wants to imprison one in the suburbs.

GRIBSBY Quite so, quite so.

ALGERNON By the way, Gribsby: Gribsby, you are not to go back to the station in that cab. That is my cab. It was taken for my convenience. You have got to walk to the station. And a very good thing, too. Solicitors don't walk nearly enough. I don't know any Solicitor who takes sufficient exercise. As a rule they sit in stuffy offices all day long neglecting their business.

JACK You can take the cab, Mr Gribsby.

GRIBSBY Thank you, sir.

Exit.

CECILY The day is getting very sultry, isn't it, Dr Chasuble?

DR CHASUBLE There is thunder in the air.

MISS PRISM The atmosphere requires to be cleared.

DR CHASUBLE Have you read the *Times* this morning, Mr Worthing? There is a very interesting article on the growth of religious feeling among the laity.

JACK I am keeping it for after dinner.

Enter MERRIMAN.

MERRIMAN Luncheon is on the table, sir.

ALGERNON Ah! that is good news. I am excessively hungry.

CECILY *(interposing)* But you have lunched already.

JACK Lunched already?

CECILY Yes, Uncle Jack. He had some pâté de foie gras sandwiches, and a small bottle of that champagne that your doctor ordered for you.

JACK My '74 champagne!

CECILY Yes. I thought you would like him to have the same one as yourself.

JACK Oh! well, if he has lunched once, he can't be expected to lunch twice. It would be absurd.

MISS PRISM To partake of two luncheons in one day would not be liberty. It would be licence.

DR CHASUBLE Even the pagan philosophers condemned excess in eating, Aristotle speaks of it with severity. He uses the same terms about it as he does about usury.

JACK Doctor, will you escort the ladies into luncheon?

DR CHASUBLE With pleasure.

He goes into the house with MISS PRISM *and* CECILY.

JACK Your Bunburying has not been a great success after all, Algy. I don't think it is a good day for Bunburying, myself.

ALGERNON Oh! there are ups and downs in Bunburying, just as there are in everything else. I'd be all right if you would let me have some lunch. The main thing is that I have seen Cecily and she is a darling.

JACK You are not to talk of Miss Cardew like that. And you are not going to have any luncheon. You have lunched already.

ALGERNON I only had some champagne and one or two sandwiches.

JACK Yes, my champagne and one or two of my sandwiches.

ALGERNON Well, I don't like your clothes. You look perfectly ridiculous in them. There is no use in being in mourning for me any longer. I have never been in better health than I am in at the present moment. Why on earth don't you go up and change? It is perfectly childish to be in deep mourning for a man who is actually staying for a whole week with you in your house as a guest.

JACK You are certainly not staying with me for a whole week as a guest or anything else. You have got to leave.

ALGERNON I certainly won't leave you so long as you are in mourning. It would be most unfriendly. If I were in mourning you would stay with me, I suppose. I should think it very unkind if you didn't.

JACK Well, will you go if I change my clothes?

ALGERNON Yes, if you are not too long. I never saw anybody take so long to dress, and with such little result.

JACK Well, at any rate, that is better than being always over-dressed as you are.

ALGERNON If I am occasionally a little over-dressed, I make up for it by being always immensely over-educated.

JACK Your vanity is ridiculous, your conduct an outrage, and your presence in my garden utterly absurd. However, you have got to catch the three-fifty, and I hope you will have a pleasant journey back to town. This Bunburying, as you call it, has not been a great success for you.

Exit.

ALGERNON I think it has been a great success. I'm in love with Cecily, and that is everything. It is all very well, but one can't Bunbury when one is hungry. I think I'll join them at lunch. *(Goes towards the door)*

Enter CECILY.

CECILY I promised Uncle Jack that I wouldn't speak to you again, unless you asked me a question. I can't understand why you don't ask me a question of some kind. I am afraid you are not quite so intellectual as I thought you were at first.

ALGERNON Cecily, mayn't I come in to lunch?

CECILY I wonder you can look me in the face after your conduct.

ALGERNON I love looking you in the face.

CECILY But why did you try to put your horrid bill on poor Uncle Jack? I think that was inexcusable of you.

ALGERNON I know it was: but the fact is I have a most wretched memory. I quite forgot I owed the Savoy £762 14s. 2d.

CECILY Well, I admit I am glad to hear that you have a bad memory. Good memories are not a quality that women admire much in men.

ALGERNON Cecily, I am fearfully hungry.

CECILY I can't understand your being so hungry, considering all you have had to eat since last October.

ALGERNON Oh! those suppers were for poor Bunbury. Late suppers are the only things his doctor allows him to eat.

CECILY Well, I don't wonder then that Mr Bunbury is always so ill, if he eats supper for six or eight people every night of the week.

ALGERNON That is what I always tell him. But he seems to think his doctors know best. He's perfectly silly about doctors.

CECILY Of course I don't want you to starve, so I have told the butler to send you out some lunch.

ALGERNON Cecily, what a perfect angel you are! May I not see you again before I go?

CECILY Miss Prism and I will be here after lunch. I always have my afternoon lessons under the yew-tree.

ALGERNON Can't you invent something to get Miss Prism out of the way?

CECILY Do you mean invent a falsehood?

ALGERNON Oh! not a falsehood, of course. Simply something that is not quite true, but should be.

CECILY I am afraid I couldn't possibly do that. I shouldn't know how. People never think of cultivating a young girl's imagination. It is the great defect of modern education. Of course, if you happened to mention that dear Dr Chasuble was waiting somewhere to see Miss Prism, she would certainly go to meet him. She never likes to keep him waiting. And she has so few opportunities of doing so.

ALGERNON What a capital suggestion!

CECILY I didn't suggest anything, Cousin Ernest. Nothing would induce me to deceive Miss Prism in the smallest detail. I merely pointed out that if you adopted a certain line of conduct, a certain result would follow.

ALGERNON Of course. I beg your pardon, Cousin Cecily. Then I shall come here at half past three. I have something very serious to say to you.

CECILY Serious?

ALGERNON Yes: very serious.

CECILY In that case, I think we had better meet in the house. I don't like talking seriously in the open air. It looks so artificial.

ALGERNON Then where shall we meet?

Enter **JACK**.

JACK The dog-cart is at the door. You have got to go. Your place is by Bunbury. *(Sees* **CECILY***)* Cecily! Don't you think, Cecily, that you had better return to Miss Prism and Dr Chasuble?

CECILY Yes, Uncle Jack. Good-bye, Cousin Ernest. I am afraid I shan't see you again, as I shall be doing my lessons with Miss Prism in the drawing-room at half past three.

ALGERNON Good-bye, Cousin Cecily. You have been very kind to me.

Exit **CECILY**.

JACK Now look here, Algy. You have got to go, and the sooner you go the better. Bunbury is extremely ill, and your place is by his side.

ALGERNON I can't go at the present moment. I must first just have my second lunch. And you will be pleased to hear that Bunbury is very much better.

JACK Well, you will have to go at three-fifty, at any rate. I ordered your things to be packed and the dog-cart to come round.

Act drop.

ACT III

SCENE: Sitting-room at the Manor House.

CECILY *and* **MISS PRISM** *discovered; each writing at a separate table.*

MISS PRISM Cecily! *(CECILY makes no answer)* Cecily! You are again making entries in your diary. I think I have had occasion more than once to speak to you about that morbid habit of yours.

CECILY I am merely, as I always do, taking you for my example, Miss Prism.

MISS PRISM When one has thoroughly mastered the principles of Bimetallism one has a right to lead an introspective life. Hardly before. I must beg you to return to your Political Economy.

CECILY In one moment, dear Miss Prism. The fact is I have only chronicled the events of to-day up till two-fifteen, and it was at two-thirty that the fearful catastrophe occurred.

MISS PRISM Pardon me, Cecily, it was exactly at one-forty-five that Dr Chasuble mentioned the very painful views held by the Primitive Church on Marriage.

CECILY I was not referring to Dr Chasuble at all. I was alluding to the tragic exposure of poor Mr Ernest Worthing.

MISS PRISM I highly disapprove of Mr Ernest Worthing. He is a thoroughly bad young man.

CECILY I fear he must be. It is the only explanation I can find for his strange attractiveness.

MISS PRISM *(rising)* Cecily, let me entreat of you not to be led away by whatever superficial qualities this unfortunate young man may possess.

CECILY Ah! believe me, dear Miss Prism, it is only the superficial qualities that last. Man's deeper nature is soon found out.

MISS PRISM Child! I do not know where you get such ideas. They are certainly not to be found in any of the improving books that I have procured for you.

CECILY Are there ever any ideas in improving books? I fear not. I get my ideas...in the garden.

MISS PRISM Then you should certainly not be so much in the open air. The fact is, you have fallen lately, Cecily, into a bad habit of thinking for yourself. You should give it up. It is not quite womanly... Men don't like it.

Enter ALGERNON *right centre.*

Mr Worthing, I thought, I may say I was in hopes that you had already returned to town.

ALGERNON My departure will not long be delayed. I have come to bid you good-bye, Miss Cardew. I am informed that a dog-cart has been already ordered for me. I have no option but to go back again into the cold world.

CECILY I hardly know, Mr Worthing, what you can mean by using such an expression. The day, even for the month of July, is unusually warm.

MISS PRISM Profligacy is apt to dull the senses.

ALGERNON No doubt. I am far from defending the weather. I think, however, that it is only my duty to mention to you, Miss Prism, that Dr Chasuble is expecting you in the vestry.

MISS PRISM In the vestry! That sounds serious. It can hardly be for any trivial purpose that the Rector selects for an interview a place of such peculiarly solemn associations. I do not think that it would be right to keep him waiting, Cecily?

CECILY It would be very, very wrong. The vestry is, I am told, excessively damp,

MISS PRISM True! I had not thought of that, and Dr Chasuble is sadly rheumatic. Mr Worthing, we shall probably not meet again. You will allow me, I trust, to express a sincere hope that you will now turn over a new leaf in life.

ALGERNON I have already begun an entire volume, Miss Prism.

MISS PRISM I am delighted to hear it. *(Puts on a large unbecoming hat)* And do not forget that there is always hope even for the most depraved. Do not be idle, Cecily.

CECILY I have no intention of being idle. I realise only too strongly that I have a great deal of serious work before me.

MISS PRISM Ah! that is quite as it should be, dear.

Exit MISS PRISM.

ALGERNON *(after a pause)* This parting, Miss Cardew, is very painful.

CECILY It is always painful to part from people whom one has known for a very brief space of time. The absence of old friends one can endure with equanimity. But even a momentary separation from anyone to whom one has just been introduced is almost unbearable.

ALGERNON Thank you.

Enter MERRIMAN.

MERRIMAN The dog-cart is at the door, sir.

ALGERNON *looks at* CECILY *appealingly.*

CECILY It can wait, Merriman. (ALGERNON *smiles,* CECILY *frowns and says in a severe voice)* For five minutes.

MERRIMAN Yes, miss.

Exit.

ALGERNON *(pulls out his watch)* Miss Cardew, I hope I shall not offend you if I state quite frankly and openly that you seem to me to be in every way the visible personification of absolute perfection.

CECILY   I think your frankness does you great credit, Mr Worthing. If you will allow me I will copy your remarks into my diary. *(Goes over to table and begins writing in diary)*

ALGERNON *(following over)* Do you really keep a diary? I'd give anything to look at it. May I?

CECILY Oh no! *(Puts her hand over it)* You see it is simply a very young girl's record of her own thoughts and impressions, and consequently meant for publication. When it appears in volume form I hope you will order a copy. But pray, Mr Worthing, don't stop. I delight in taking down from dictation. I have reached "absolute perfection". You can go on. I am quite ready for more.

ALGERNON *(somewhat taken aback)* Ahem! ...Ahcm!

CECILY Oh, don't cough, Mr Worthing. When one is dictating one should speak fluently, and not cough. Besides, I don't know how to spell a cough.

ALGERNON *(speaking very rapidly)* Miss Cardew, ever since half past twelve this afternoon, when I first looked upon your wonderful and incomparable beauty, I have not merely been your abject slave and servant, but, soaring upon the pinions of a possibly monstrous ambition, I have dared to love you wildly, passionately, devotedly, hopelessly.

CECILY *(laying down her pen)* Oh! please say that all over again. You speak far too fast and far too indistinctly. Kindly say it all over again.

ALGERNON Miss Cardew, ever since you were half past twelve—I mean ever since it was half past twelve, this afternoon, when I first looked upon your wonderful and incomparable beauty...

CECILY Yes, I have got that, all right.

ALGERNON *(stammering)* I—I—

CECILY *lays down her pen and looks reproachfully at him.*

(desperately) I have not merely been your abject slave and servant, but, soaring on the pinions of a possibly monstrous ambition, I have dared to love you wildly, passionately, devotedly, hopelessly. *(Takes out his watch and looks at it)*

CECILY *(after writing for some time, looks up)* I have not taken down "hopelessly". It doesn't seem to make much sense, does it? *(A slight pause)*

ALGERNON *(starting back)* Cecily!

CECILY Is that the beginning of an entirely new paragraph? or should it be followed by a note of admiration?

ALGERNON *(rapidly and romantically)* It is the beginning of an entirely new existence for me, and it shall be followed by such notes of admiration that my whole life shall be a subtle and sustained symphony of Love, Praise and Adoration combined.

CECILY Oh, I don't think that makes any sense at all. The fact is that men should never try to dictate to women. They never know how to do it, and when they do do it, they always say something particularly foolish.

ALGERNON I don't care whether what I say is foolish or not. All that I know is that I love you, Cecily. I love you, I want you. I can't live without you, Cecily! You know I love you. Will you marry me? Will you be my wife? *(Rushes over to her and puts his hand on hers)*

CECILY *(rising)* Oh, you have made me make a blot! And yours is the only real proposal I have ever had in all my life. I should like to have entered it neatly.

Enter MERRIMAN.

MERRIMAN The dog-cart is waiting, sir.

ALGERNON Tell it to come round next week at the same hour.

MERRIMAN (*looks at* CECILY *who makes no sign*) Yes, sir.

Exit.

CECILY Uncle Jack would be very much annoyed if he knew you were staying on till next week, at the same hour.

ALGERNON Oh! I don't care about Jack! I don't care for anybody in the whole world but you. I love you. Cecily! you will marry me, won't you?

CECILY You silly boy! Of course. Why we have been engaged for the last five months.

ALGERNON For the last five months?

CECILY Five months all but a few days. (*Looks at diary turns over page*) Yes; it will be exactly five months on Thursday.

ALGERNON I didn't know.

CECILY Very few people nowadays ever realise the position in which they are placed. The age is, as Miss Prism often says, a thoughtless one.

ALGERNON But how did we become engaged?

CECILY Well, ever since dear Uncle Jack first confessed to us that he had a younger brother who was very wicked and bad, you of course have formed the chief topic of conversation between myself and Miss Prism. And of course a man who is much talked about is always very attractive. One feels there must be something in him, after all. I dare say it was foolish of me, but I fell in love with you, Ernest.

ALGERNON Darling! But when was the engagement actually settled?

CECILY On the 14th of February last. Worn out by your entire ignorance of my existence I determined to end the matter one way or the other, and after a long struggle with myself

I accepted you one evening in the garden. The next day I bought this little ring in your name. You see I always wear it, Ernest, and though it shows that you are sadly extravagant, still I have long ago forgiven you for that. Here in this drawer are all the little presents I have given you from time to time, neatly numbered and labelled. This is the pearl necklace you gave me on my birthday. And this is the box in which I keep all your letters. *(Opens box and produces letters tied up with blue ribbon)*

ALGERNON My letters! But my own sweet Cecily, I have never written you any letters.

CECILY You need hardly remind me of that, Ernest. I remember it only too well. I grew tired of asking the postman every morning if he had a London letter for me. My health began to give way under the strain and anxiety. So I wrote your letters for you, and had them posted to me in the village by my maid. I wrote always three times a week and sometimes oftener.

ALGERNON Oh, do let me read them, Cecily.

CECILY Oh, I couldn't possibly. They would make you far too conceited. The three you wrote me after I had broken off the engagement are so beautiful and so badly spelt that even now I can hardly read them without crying a little.

ALGERNON But was our engagement ever broken off?

CECILY Of course it was. On the 22nd of last March. You can see the entry if you like. *(Shows diary)* "To-day I broke off my engagement with Ernest. I feel it is better to do so. The weather still continues charming."

ALGERNON But why on earth did you break it off? What had I done? I had done nothing at all. Cecily, I am very much hurt, indeed, to hear you broke it off. Particularly when the weather was so charming.

CECILY Men seem to forget very easily. I should have thought you would have remembered the violent letter you wrote to me because I danced with Lord Kelso at the county ball.

ALGERNON But I did take it all back, Cecily, didn't I?

CECILY Of course you did. Otherwise I wouldn't have forgiven you or accepted this little gold bangle with the turquoise and diamond heart, that you sent me the next day. *(Shows bangle)*

ALGERNON Did I give you this, Cecily? It's very pretty, isn't it?

CECILY Yes: you have wonderfully good taste, Ernest. I have always said that of you. It's the excuse I've always given for your leading such a bad life.

ALGERNON My own one! So we have been engaged for five months, Cecily!

CECILY Yes; how the time has flown, hasn't it?

ALGERNON I don't think so. I have found the days very long and very dreary without you.

CECILY You dear romantic boy... *(Puts her fingers through his hair)* I hope your hair curls naturally. Does it?

ALGERNON Yes, darling.

CECILY I am so glad.

A pause.

ALGERNON You'll never break off our engagement again, Cecily?

CECILY I don't think I could break it off now that I have met you. Besides, of course there is the question of your name.

ALGERNON How do you mean?

CECILY You must not laugh at me, darling, but it had always been a girlish dream of mine to love someone whose name was Ernest. There is something in that name that seems to inspire absolute confidence. I pity any married woman whose husband is not called Ernest.

ALGERNON But, my dear child, do you mean to say you could not love me if I had some other name?

CECILY But you have no other name.

ALGERNON That is quite true. But supposing that my godfathers and godmother had given me some other name?

CECILY But what name?

ALGERNON Oh! any name you like—Algernon, for instance.

CECILY But I don't like the name of Algernon.

ALGERNON Well, my own sweet darling, I really can't see why you should object to the name of Algernon. It is not at all a bad name. In fact it is rather an aristocratic name.

CECILY I fear it must be. I have often come across it in the newspapers in connection with rather painful cases—cases that judges and magistrates have had to decide unfairly.

ALGERNON Oh! of course there are Algies and Algies: but I know lots of Algies who are very respectable Algies.

CECILY Oh! I don't think I would like those Algies at all.

ALGERNON But seriously, Cecily, if my name was Algy, couldn't you love me?

CECILY I might respect you, Ernest, I might admire your character. But I fear that I would not be able to give you my undivided attention.

ALGERNON How perfectly terrible!

CECILY Why, Ernest?

ALGERNON Oh, nothing, darling. Ahem! —Cecily, your Rector here is, I suppose, thoroughly experienced in the practice of all the rites and ceremonials of the Church?

CECILY Oh yes! Dr Chasuble is a most learned man. He has never written a single book, so you can imagine how much he knows.

ALGERNON I must see him at once on a most important christening—I mean on most important business.

CECILY *(pained)* Oh!

ALGERNON I shan't be away more than half an hour, darling.

CECILY Considering that we have been engaged since February the 14th, and that I only met you to-day for the first time, I think it is rather hard that you should leave me for so long a period as half an hour. Couldn't you make it twenty minutes?

ALGERNON I'll be back in no time.

Kisses her and rushes out.

CECILY Dear sweet boy he is! I like his hair so much! I must enter his proposal in my diary! *(Goes over to table and sits down)*

Enter MERRIMAN.

MERRIMAN A Miss Fairfax has just called to see Mr Worthing on very important business.

CECILY Is Mr Worthing not in his library?

MERRIMAN Mr Worthing went over in the direction of the Rectory some time ago.

CECILY Oh! Pray show the lady in. Mr Worthing is sure to be back soon. And you can bring tea.

MERRIMAN Yes, miss.

Exit.

CECILY Miss Fairfax! I suppose one of the many good women who are associated with Uncle Jack in some of his philanthropic work in London. I don't quite like women who are interested in philanthropic work. I think it is so forward of them. Perhaps she is not a good woman at all, perhaps she is only a New woman. I don't like these New women, they are so old.

Enter MERRIMAN.

MERRIMAN Miss Fairfax.

Enter **GWENDOLEN**.

Exit **MERRIMAN**.

CECILY *(advancing to meet her)* Pray let me introduce myself to you. My name is Cecily Cardew.

GWENDOLEN Cecily Cardew? What a very sweet name! Something tells me that we are going to be great friends. I like you already more than I can say. My first impressions of people are never wrong.

CECILY How nice of you to like me so much after we have known each other such a comparatively short time. Pray sit down!

GWENDOLEN *(still standing up)* I may call you Cecily, may I not?

CECILY With pleasure!

GWENDOLEN And you will always call me Gwendolen, won't you?

CECILY If you wish.

GWENDOLEN *(sitting down)* Then that is all quite settled, is it not?

CECILY I hope so. *(A pause)*

GWENDOLEN Perhaps this would not be a bad opportunity for my mentioning who I am. My father is Lord Bracknell. You have never heard of Papa, I suppose?

CECILY I don't think so.

GWENDOLEN Outside the family circle Papa, I am glad to say, is entirely unknown. I think that is quite as it should be. The home seems to me to be the proper sphere for the man. And certainly once a man begins to neglect his domestic duties he becomes painfully effeminate, does he not? And I don't like that. It makes men so very attractive... Mamma, whose views on education are remarkably strict, has brought me up to be extremely shortsighted; it is part of her system, so do you mind my looking at you through my glasses?

CECILY Not at all, Gwendolen. I am very fond of being looked at.

GWENDOLEN *(after examining* CECILY *carefully through a lorgnette)* You are here on a short visit, I suppose?

CECILY Oh no; I live here.

GWENDOLEN *(severely)* Really? Your mother, no doubt, or some female relative of advanced years, resides here also?

CECILY Oh no! I have no mother, nor in fact any relations.

GWENDOLEN Indeed?

CECILY My dear guardian, with the assistance of Miss Prism, has the arduous task of looking after me.

GWENDOLEN Your guardian?

CECILY Yes: I am Mr Worthing's ward.

GWENDOLEN Oh! It is strange he never mentioned to me that he had a ward. How secretive of him! He grows more interesting hourly! I am not sure, however, that the news inspires me with feelings of unmixed delight. I am very fond of you, Cecily: I have liked you ever since I met you: but I am bound to state that now that I know that you are Mr Worthing's ward, I cannot help expressing the wish you were—well, just a little older than you seem to be—and not quite so very alluring in appearance. In fact, if I may speak candidly?

CECILY Pray do. I think that whenever one has anything unpleasant to say one should always be quite candid—

GWENDOLEN Well, to speak candidly, Cecily, I wish that you were fully thirty-five and more than usually plain for your age. Ernest has a strong upright nature. He is the very soul of truth and honour. But even men of the noblest possible moral character are extremely susceptible to the influence of the physical charms of others.

CECILY I beg your pardon, Gwendolen, did you say Ernest?

GWENDOLEN Yes.

CECILY Oh, but it is not Mr Ernest Worthing who is my guardian. It is his brother—his elder brother.

GWENDOLEN Ernest never mentioned to me that he had a brother.

CECILY I am sorry to say they have not been on good terms for a long time.

GWENDOLEN Ah! that accounts for it. And now that I think of it I have never heard any man mention his brother. The subject seems distasteful to most men. Cecily, you have lifted a load from my mind. I was growing almost anxious. It would have been terrible if any cloud had come across a friendship like ours—would it not? Of course you are quite, quite sure that it is not Mr Ernest Worthing who is your guardian?

CECILY Quite sure. *(A pause)* In fact I am going to be his.

GWENDOLEN *(inquiringly)* I beg your pardon?

CECILY *(rather shyly and confidingly)* Dearest Gwendolen, there is no reason why I should make any secret of it to you. Our little county newspaper is sure to chronicle the fact next week. Mr Ernest Worthing and I are engaged to be married.

GWENDOLEN *(quite politely, rising)* My darling Cecily, I think there must be some slight error. Mr Ernest Worthing is engaged to me. The announcement will appear in the *Morning Post* on Saturday at the latest.

CECILY *(very politely, rising)* I am afraid you must be under some misconception. Ernest proposed to me exactly ten minutes ago. *(Shows diary)*

GWENDOLEN *(examines diary through her lorgnette carefully)* It is certainly very curious. For he asked me to be his wife yesterday afternoon at five-thirty. If you would care to verify the incident, pray do so. *(Produces diary of her own)* I never travel without my diary. One should always have something sensational to read in a train. I am so sorry, dear Cecily, if it is any disappointment to you, but I am afraid I have the prior claim.

CECILY It would distress me more than I can tell you, dear Gwendolen, if it caused you any mental or physical anguish, but I feel bound to point out that since Ernest proposed to you he has clearly changed his mind.

GWENDOLEN *(meditatively)* If the poor fellow has been entrapped into any foolish promise, I will consider it my duty to rescue him at once, and with a firm hand.

CECILY *(thoughtfully and sadly)* Whatever unfortunate entanglement my dear boy may have got into, I will never reproach him with it, after we are married.

GWENDOLEN Do you allude to me, Miss Cardew, as an entanglement? You are presumptuous. On an occasion of this kind it becomes more than a moral duty to speak one's mind. It becomes a pleasure.

CECILY Do you suggest, Miss Fairfax, that I entrapped Ernest into an engagement? How dare you? This is no time for wearing the shallow mask of manners. When I see a spade I call it a spade.

GWENDOLEN *(satirically)* I am glad to say that I have never seen a spade. It is obvious that our social spheres have been widely different.

CECILY *is about to make a retort when* MERRIMAN *enters, followed by a* FOOTMAN *with tea tray, etc. The presence of the* SERVANTS *exercises a restraining influence under which both girls chafe.*

MERRIMAN Shall I lay tea here as usual, miss?

CECILY *(sternly, in a clear voice)* Yes. As usual.

MERRIMAN *lays tea on table close to* CECILY. *A long pause,* CECILY *and* GWENDOLEN *glare at each other.*

GWENDOLEN *(looking round)* Quite a charming room this is of yours, Miss Cardew.

CECILY So glad you like it, Miss Fairfax.

GWENDOLEN I had no idea there was anything approaching good taste in the more remote country districts. It is quite a surprise to me.

CECILY I am afraid you judge of the country from what one sees in town. I believe most London houses are extremely vulgar.

GWENDOLEN I suppose they do dazzle the rural mind. Personally I cannot understand how anybody manages to exist in the country—if anybody who is anybody does. The country always bores me to death.

CECILY Ah! that is what the newspapers call agricultural depression, is it not? I believe the aristocracy are suffering very much from it just at present. It is almost an epidemic amongst them, I have been told. May I offer you some tea, Miss Fairfax?

GWENDOLEN *(with elaborate politeness)* Thank you. *(Aside)* Detestable girl! But I require tea.

CECILY *(sweetly)* Sugar? *(Holds up tongs)*

GWENDOLEN *(superciliously)* No, thank you. (CECILY *puts down tongs)* Sugar is not fashionable any more.

CECILY *looks angrily at her, takes up tongs again and puts four lumps of sugar into the cup.*

CECILY *(severely)* Cake, or bread and butter?

GWENDOLEN *(in a bored manner)* Bread and butter, please. (CECILY *puts bread and butter on tray)* Cake is rarely seen at the best houses nowadays.

CECILY *cuts a very large slice of cake, removes the bread and butter, and puts the slice of cake on the tray.*

CECILY (*to* MERRIMAN *who is waiting with a small salver on which the cup of tea stands*) Hand that to Miss Fairfax. (MERRIMAN *hands the salver*) That will do, Merriman.

Exit MERRIMAN *with* FOOTMAN.

GWENDOLEN (*drinks the tea and makes a grimace and puts the cup down at once, reaches out her hand to the bread and butter, looks at it, and finds it is cake. Rises in indignation*) You have filled my tea with lumps of sugar, and though I asked most distinctly for bread and butter you have given me cake. I am known for the gentleness of my disposition, and the extraordinary sweetness of my nature, but I warn you, Miss Cardew, you may go too far.

CECILY (*rising*) To save my poor innocent trusting boy from the machinations of any other girl there are no lengths to which I would not go.

GWENDOLEN From the moment I saw you I distrusted you. I felt that you were false and deceitful. I am never deceived in such matters. My first impressions of people are invariably right.

CECILY It seems to me, Miss Fairfax, that I am trespassing on your valuable time. No doubt you have many other calls of a similar character to make in the neighbourhood.

Enter JACK *behind.*

GWENDOLEN (*catching sight of him*) Ernest! My own Ernest!

JACK (*advancing*) Gwendolen! Darling! (*Offers to kiss her*)

GWENDOLEN (*drawing back*) A moment! May I ask if you are engaged to be married to this young lady? (*Points to* CECILY)

JACK (*laughing*) To dear little Cecily! Of course not. What could have put such an idea into your pretty little head?

GWENDOLEN Thank you. You may. (*Offers her cheek*)

CECILY (*very sweetly*) I knew there must be some misunderstanding, Miss Fairfax. The gentleman whose arm is at present round your waist is my dear guardian, Mr John Worthing.

GWENDOLEN I beg your pardon?

CECILY This is Uncle Jack.

GWENDOLEN *(receding)* Jack! Oh!

Enter **ALGERNON**.

CECILY Here is Ernest!

ALGERNON *(goes straight over to* **CECILY** *without noticing anyone else)* My own love! *(Offers to kiss her)*

CECILY *(drawing back)* Ernest, may I ask if you are engaged to be married to this young lady?

ALGERNON *(looking round)* To what young lady? Good heavens! Gwendolen!

CECILY Yes: to good heavens Gwendolen. I mean to Gwendolen!

ALGERNON *(laughing)* Of course not. What could have put such an idea into your pretty, little head?

CECILY Thank you. *(Presenting her cheek to be kissed)* You may. *(***ALGERNON** *kisses her)*

GWENDOLEN I felt there was some slight error, Miss Cardew. The gentleman who is now embracing you is my cousin, Mr Algernon Moncrieff.

CECILY *(breaking away from* **ALGERNON***)* Algernon Moncrieff! Oh!

The two girls come towards each other and put their arms round each other's waists, as if for protection.

(to **ALGERNON***)* Are you called Algernon?

ALGERNON *(flinging himself in despair on the sofa)* I cannot deny it!

CECILY Oh!

GWENDOLEN Is your name really John?

JACK *(standing rather proudly)* I could deny it if I liked. I could deny anything if I liked. But my name certainly is John. It has been John for years.

CECILY *(to* GWENDOLEN*)* A gross deception has been practised on both of us.

GWENDOLEN My poor wounded Cecily!

CECILY My sweet wronged Gwendolen!

GWENDOLEN *(slowly and seriously)* You will call me sister, will you not?

CECILY *(after a pause)* Thank you for those words.

They kiss.

(rather brightly) There is just one question I would like to be allowed to ask my guardian.

GWENDOLEN An admirable idea! Mr Worthing, there is just one question I would like to be permitted to put to you. Where is your brother Ernest? We are both engaged to be married to your brother Ernest, so it is a matter of some importance to us to know where your brother Ernest is at present.

JACK *(slowly and hesitatingly)* Gwendolen—Cecily—it is very painful for me to be forced to speak the truth. It is the first time in my life that I have ever been reduced to such a painful position, and I am really quite inexperienced in doing anything of the kind, so you must excuse me if I stammer in my tale.

GWENDOLEN I must beg you to do nothing of the kind, Mr Worthing. Stammering always gets upon my nerves. Pray say what you have to say without the smallest hesitation in your speech.

JACK In that case I will tell you quite frankly that I have no brother Ernest. I have no brother at all. I never had a brother in my life, and I certainly have not the smallest intention of ever having one in the future.

CECILY *(going towards him)* No brother at all?

JACK *(cheerily)* None.

GWENDOLEN *(severely)* Had you never a brother of any kind?

JACK *(pleasantly)* Never. Not even of any kind.

GWENDOLEN Then it is quite clear, Cecily, that neither of us is engaged to be married to anyone.

CECILY It is not a very—pleasant position for a young girl suddenly to find herself in. Is it?

GWENDOLEN Let us go out into the garden. They will hardly venture to come after us there!

CECILY No: men are so cowardly, aren't they?

Exeunt into garden, with scornful looks.

JACK *and* ALGERNON *look at each other for a short time, then turn away from each other.* JACK, *who looks very angry, walks up and down the room, kicks a footstool aside in a very irritated way.* ALGERNON *goes over to tea table and eats some muffins after lifting up the covers of several dishes.*

JACK Pretty mess you have got me into.

ALGERNON *sits down at tea table and pours out some tea. He seems quite unconcerned.*

What on earth did you mean by coming down here and pretending to be my brother? Perfectly monstrous of you!

ALGERNON *(eating muffin)* What on earth did you mean by pretending to have a brother? It was absolutely disgraceful! *(Eats another muffin)*

JACK I told you to go away by the three-fifty. I ordered the dog-cart for you. Why on earth didn't you take it?

ALGERNON I hadn't had my tea.

JACK This ghastly state of things is what you call Bunburying, I suppose?

ALGERNON Yes, and a perfectly wonderful Bunbury it is. The most wonderful Bunbury I have ever had in my life.

JACK Well, you've no right whatsoever to Bunbury in my house.

ALGERNON That is absurd. One has a right to Bunbury anywhere one chooses. Every serious Bunburyist knows that.

JACK Serious Bunburyist! Good heavens!

ALGERNON Well, one must be serious about something, if one wants to have any amusement in life. I happen to be serious about Bunburying. What on earth you are serious about I haven't got the remotest idea. About everything I should fancy. You have such an absolutely trivial nature.

JACK Well the only small satisfaction I have in the whole of this wretched business is that your friend Bunbury is quite exploded. You won't be able to run down to the country quite so often as you used to do, dear Algy. And a very good thing, too.

ALGERNON Your brother is a little off colour, isn't he, dear Jack? You won't be able to disappear to London quite as frequently as your wicked custom was. And not a bad thing either.

JACK As for your conduct towards Miss Cardew, I must say that your taking in a sweet, simple, innocent girl like that is quite inexcusable. To say nothing of the fact that she is my ward.

ALGERNON I can see no possible defence at all for your deceiving a brilliant, clever, thoroughly experienced young lady like Miss Fairfax. To say nothing of the fact that she is my cousin.

JACK I wanted to be engaged to Gwendolen, that is all. I love her.

ALGERNON Well, I simply wanted to be engaged to Cecily. I adore her.

JACK There is certainly no chance of your marrying Miss Cardew.

ALGERNON I don't think there is much likelihood, Jack, of you and Miss Fairfax being united.

JACK Well, that is no business of yours.

ALGERNON If it was my business I wouldn't talk about it. It is very vulgar to talk about one's business. Only people like stockbrokers do that, and then merely at dinner parties.

JACK How you can sit there, calmly eating muffins, when we are in this horrible trouble, I can't make out. You seem to me to be perfectly heartless.

ALGERNON Well, I can't eat muffins in an agitated manner. The butter would probably get on my cuffs. One should always eat muffins quite calmly. It is the only way to eat them.

JACK I say it is perfectly heartless your eating muffins at all, under the circumstances.

ALGERNON When I am in trouble, eating is the only thing that consoles me. Indeed, when I am in really great trouble, as anyone who knows me intimately will tell you, I refuse everything, except food and drink. At the present moment I am eating muffins because I am unhappy. Besides, I am particularly fond of muffins.

JACK *(going over to tea table and sitting down)* Well, that is no reason why you should eat them all in that greedy way. *(Helps himself to muffin)*

ALGERNON *(offering tea-cake)* I wish you would have tea-cake, instead. I don't like tea-cake.

JACK Good heavens! I suppose a man may eat his own muffins in his own house!

ALGERNON But you have just said it was perfectly heartless to eat muffins.

JACK I said it was perfectly heartless of you under the circumstances. That is a very different thing.

ALGERNON That may be. But the muffins are the same. *(Removes muffin plate)*

JACK Algy! I wish to goodness you would leave my house—I don't want you here. What on earth are you staying for?

ALGERNON I have not finished my tea yet. And after that, I have got to be baptised. I have a heap of things to get through before dinner. What time, by the way, do we dine, Jack—eight?

JACK I have not invited you to dinner. I won't let you stay to dinner. You have got to go.

ALGERNON You can't possibly ask me to go without having some dinner. It is absurd. I never go without my dinner. No one ever does, except vegetarians and people like that.

JACK What on earth do you mean by talking about being baptised after tea?

ALGERNON I have just made arrangements with Dr Chasuble to be baptised at a quarter to six under the name of Ernest.

JACK My dear fellow, the sooner you give up that nonsense, the better. I made arrangements this morning with Dr Chasuble to be baptised myself at five-thirty, and I naturally will take the name of Ernest. Gwendolen would wish it. We can't both be christened Ernest. It'd be absurd. Besides, I have a perfect right to be baptised, if I like. There is no evidence at all that I ever have been baptised by anybody. I should think it extremely probable I never was and so does Dr Chasuble. It is entirely different in your case. You have been baptised already.

ALGERNON Yes, but I have not been baptised for years.

JACK Yes, but you have been baptised. That is the important thing.

ALGERNON Quite so. So I know my constitution can stand it. If you are not quite sure about your ever having been baptised, I must say I think it rather dangerous your venturing on it now. It might make you very unwell. You can hardly have forgotten that someone very closely connected with you was very nearly carried off this week in Paris by a severe chill.

JACK   Yes; but you said yourself it was not hereditary, or anything of the kind.

ALGERNON   It usen't to be, I know—but I dare say it is now. Science is always making wonderful improvements in things.

JACK   May I ask, Algy, what on earth do you propose to do?

ALGERNON   Nothing. That is what I have been trying to do for the last ten minutes, and you have kept on doing everything in your power to distract my attention from my work.

JACK   Well, I shall go out into the garden, and see Gwendolen. I feel quite sure she expects me.

ALGERNON   I know from her extremely cold manner that Cecily expects me so I certainly shan't go out into the garden. When a man does exactly what a woman expects him to do, she doesn't think much of him. One should always do what a woman doesn't expect, just as one should always say what she doesn't understand. The result is invariably perfect sympathy on both sides.

JACK   Oh, that is nonsense. You are always talking nonsense.

ALGERNON   It is much cleverer to talk nonsense than to listen to it, my dear fellow, and a much rarer thing too, in spite of all the public may say.

JACK   I don't listen to you. I can't listen to you.

ALGERNON   Oh, that is merely false modesty. You know perfectly well you could listen to me if you tried. You always under-rate yourself, an absurd thing to do nowadays when there are such a lot of conceited people about. Jack, you are eating the muffins again! I wish you wouldn't. There are only two left. (*Removes plate*) I told you I was particularly fond of muffins.

JACK   But I hate tea-cake.

ALGERNON Why on earth do you allow tea-cake to be served up to your guests, then? What ideas you have of hospitality!

JACK *(irritably)* Oh! that is not the point. We are not discussing tea-cakes. *(Crosses)* Algy! you are perfectly maddening. You never can stick to the point in any conversation.

ALGERNON *(slowly)* No: it always hurts me.

JACK Good heavens! What affectation! I loathe affectation.

ALGERNON Well, my dear fellow, if you don't like affectation, I really don't see what you can like. Besides, it isn't affectation. The point always does hurt me, and I hate physical pain, of any kind.

JACK *(glares at* **ALGERNON***; walks up and down stage. Finally comes up to table)* Algy! I have already told you to go. I don't want you here. Why don't you go?

ALGERNON I haven't quite finished my tea yet. And there is still one muffin left. *(Takes the last muffin)*

JACK *groans and sinks down into a chair and buries his face in his hands.*

Act drop.

ACT IV

SCENE: The Same.

JACK *and* **ALGERNON** *discovered in the same positions as at the close of ACT III. Enter behind,* **GWENDOLEN** *and* **CECILY.**

GWENDOLEN The fact that they did not follow us at once into the garden as anyone else would have done, seems to me to show that they have some sense of shame left.

CECILY They have been eating muffins. That looks like repentance.

They pass to front of stage.

GWENDOLEN They don't seem to notice us at all. Couldn't you cough?

CECILY But I haven't got a cough.

GWENDOLEN They're looking at us. What effrontery.

CECILY They're approaching. That's very forward of them.

GWENDOLEN Let us preserve a dignified silence.

CECILY Certainly. It's the only thing to do now.

GWENDOLEN This dignified silence does not seem to produce the desired effect.

CECILY Quite the reverse!

GWENDOLEN But we will not be the first to speak.

CECILY Certainly not.

GWENDOLEN Mr Worthing, I have something very particular to ask you. Much depends on your reply.

CECILY   Gwendolen, your commonsense is invaluable. Mr Moncrieff, kindly answer me the following question. Why did you pretend to be my guardian's brother?

ALGERNON   In order that I might have an opportunity of meeting you.

CECILY   *(to* GWENDOLEN*)* That certainly seems a satisfactory explanation, does it not?

GWENDOLEN   Yes, dear, if you can believe him.

CECILY   I don't! But that does not affect the wonderful beauty of his answer.

GWENDOLEN   True. In matters of grave importance style, not sincerity, is the vital thing. *(To* JACK*)* Mr Worthing, what explanation can you offer to me for pretending to have a brother? Was it in order that you might have an opportunity of coming up to town to see me as often as possible?

JACK   Can you doubt it, Miss Fairfax?

GWENDOLEN   I have the gravest doubts upon the subject. But I intend to crush them. This is no time for scepticism. There is too much scepticism in the age as it is. *(To* CECILY*)* Their explanations appear to be quite satisfactory, especially Mr Worthing's. That seems to me to have the stamp of truth on it.

CECILY   I am more than content with what Mr Moncrieff said. His voice alone inspires one with absolute credulity.

GWENDOLEN   Then you think we should forgive them?

CECILY   Yes. I mean no.

GWENDOLEN   True! I had forgotten. There are principles at stake that one cannot surrender. Which of us should tell them? The task is not a pleasant one.

CECILY   Could we not both speak at the same time?

GWENDOLEN   An excellent idea! I often speak at the same time as other people. Will you take the time from me?

GWENDOLEN AND CECILY *(speaking together.* **GWENDOLEN** *beats time with uplifted finger)* Your Christian names are still an absolutely insuperable barrier. That is all.

JACK AND ALGY *(speaking together)* Our Christian names! Is that all? But we are going to be christened this afternoon.

GWENDOLEN *(to* **JACK***)* For my sake you are prepared to do this terrible thing?

JACK Certainly!

CECILY *(to* **ALGERNON***)* To please me you are ready to face this fearful ordeal?

ALGERNON I am.

GWENDOLEN *(to* **CECILY***)* How absurd to talk of the equality of the sexes. Where questions of self-sacrifice are concerned, men are infinitely beyond us.

CECILY *(to* **GWENDOLEN***)* They have moments of physical courage of which we women know absolutely nothing.

JACK *(to* **GWENDOLEN***)* Darling!

ALGERNON *(to* **CECILY***)* Darling!

They fall into each other's arms.

Enter **MERRIMAN.** *When he enters he coughs loudly, seeing the situation.*

MERRIMAN Ahem! Ahem! Lady Bracknell!

JACK Good heavens!

Enter **LADY BRACKNELL**—*general consternation and scuffle.*

Exit **MERRIMAN.**

LADY BRACKNELL Gwendolen! What does this mean?

GWENDOLEN Merely that I am engaged to be married to Mr Worthing, mamma.

LADY BRACKNELL Come over here, at once.

GWENDOLEN Certainly, mamma. But I am engaged to be married to Mr Worthing.

LADY BRACKNELL Silence, child. Come here. At once. Hesitation of any kind is a sign of mental decay in the young, of physical weakness in the old. *(Turns to JACK)* Mr Worthing, apprised of my daughter's sudden flight by her trusty maid, whose confidence I purchased by means of a small coin, I followed her at once by a luggage train. Her unhappy father is, I am glad to say, under the impression that she is attending a more than usually lengthy lecture at the University Extension Scheme. I do not propose to undeceive him. Indeed I have never undeceived him on any question. I would consider it wrong. But of course you will clearly understand that all communication between yourself and my daughter must cease immediately from this moment. On this point, as indeed on all points, I am firm.

JACK I am engaged to be married to Gwendolen, Lady Bracknell.

LADY BRACKNELL You are nothing of the kind, sir. *(Turns to ALGERNON)* And now as regards Algernon! ...Algernon!

ALGERNON Yes, Aunt Augusta.

LADY BRACKNELL May I ask if it is in this house that your invalid friend Mr Bunbury resides?

ALGERNON Oh! No! Bunbury doesn't live here. Bunbury is somewhere else at present. In fact Bunbury is dead.

LADY BRACKNELL Dead? But when did Mr Bunbury die? His death must have been extremely sudden.

ALGERNON I killed Bunbury this afternoon. I mean poor Bunbury died this afternoon.

LADY BRACKNELL What did he die of?

ALGERNON Bunbury? Oh! he was quite exploded.

LADY BRACKNELL Exploded! Was he the victim of a revolutionary outrage? I was not aware that Mr Bunbury was interested in social legislation. If so, he is well punished for his morbidity.

ALGERNON My dear Aunt Augusta, I mean he was found out! The doctors found out that Bunbury could not live, that is what I mean—so Bunbury died.

LADY BRACKNELL He seems to have had great confidence in the opinion of his physicians. I am glad, however, that he made up his mind at the last to some definite course of action, and acted under proper medical advice. And now that we have buried this Mr Bunbury at last, may I ask, Mr Worthing, who is that young lady whose hand my nephew Algernon is now holding in what seems to me a peculiarly unnecessary manner?

JACK This lady, Lady Bracknell, is Miss Cecily Cardew, my ward.

LADY BRACKNELL *bows coldly to* **CECILY**.

ALGERNON I am engaged to be married to Cecily, Aunt Augusta.

LADY BRACKNELL I beg your pardon?

CECILY Mr Moncrieff and I are engaged to be married, Lady Bracknell.

LADY BRACKNELL *(with a shiver, crossing to the sofa and sitting down)* I do not know whether there is anything peculiarly exciting in the air of this part of Hertfordshire, but the amount of engagements that go on seems to me considerably above the proper average that statistics have laid down for our guidance. I think some preliminary enquiry on my part would not be out of place. Mr Worthing, is Miss Cardew at all connected with any of the larger railway stations in London? I ask merely for information. Until yesterday I had no idea that there were any families or persons, whose origin was a terminus.

JACK *looks perfectly furious, but restrains himself.*

JACK *(in a clear cold voice)* Miss Cardew is the grand-daughter of the late Mr Thomas Cardew of 149 Belgrave Square, S.W., Gervase Park, Dorking, Surrey, and the Sporran, Fifeshire, N.B.

LADY BRACKNELL That sounds not unsatisfactory. Three addresses always inspire confidence. But what proof have I of their authenticity?

*JACK gets very angry—*GWENDOLEN *makes signs to him to keep quiet—*ALGERNON *plucks at his coat tails—* CECILY *puts her hand on his arm.*

JACK *(with an elaborate bow)* I have carefully preserved the Court Guides of the Period. They are open to your inspection, Lady Bracknell.

LADY BRACKNELL *(grimly)* I have known strange errors in that publication.

JACK Miss Cardew's family solicitors are Messrs Markby, Markby, and Markby of 149a Lincoln's Inn Fields, Western Central District, London. I have no doubt they will be happy to supply you with any further information. Their office hours are from ten till four.

LADY BRACKNELL *(bowing)* Markby, Markby and Markby? A firm of the very highest position in their profession. Indeed, I am told that one of the Mr Markby's is occasionally to be seen at dinner-parties. So far I am satisfied.

JACK *(very irritably)* How extremely kind of you, Lady Bracknell! I have also in my possession, you will be pleased to hear, certificates of Miss Cardew's birth, registration, baptism, whooping-cough, vaccination, confirmation, and the measles, both the German and the English variety.

CECILY *looks reproachfully at* JACK.

LADY BRACKNELL *(calmly)* Ah! A life crowded with incident, I see; though perhaps somewhat too exciting for a young girl. I am not myself in favour of premature experiences. *(Rises and looks at her watch)* Gwendolen! the time approaches for our departure. We have not a moment to lose. As a matter of form, Mr Worthing, I had better ask you if Miss Cardew has any little fortune?

JACK Oh! about a hundred and thirty thousand pounds in the Funds. That is all. Good-bye, Lady Bracknell. So pleased to have seen you.

LADY BRACKNELL A moment, Mr Worthing. A hundred and thirty thousand! And in the Funds! *(Sitting down again)* Miss Cardew seems to me a most attractive young lady, now that I look at her. Few girls of the present day have any really solid qualities, any of the qualities that last, and improve with time. We live, I regret to say, in an age of surfaces. *(To CECILY)* Come over here, dear, (CECILY *goes across)* Pretty child! Your dress is sadly simple and your hair seems almost as Nature might have left it. But we can soon alter all that. A thoroughly experienced French maid produces a really marvellous result in a very brief space of time. I remember recommending one to young Lady Lancing, and after three months her own husband did not know her.

JACK And after six months nobody knew her.

LADY BRACKNELL *(looks angrily at JACK, but controls herself. Then bends, with a practised smile, to CECILY)* Kindly turn round, sweet child (CECILY *turns completely round)* No, the side view is what I want. (CECILY *turns her profile)* Yes, quite as I expected. There are distinct social possibilities in your profile.

CECILY Really, Lady Bracknell? How very gratifying!

LADY BRACKNELL Child! never fall into the habit, so unfortunately common nowadays, of talking trivially about serious things. The two weak points in our age are its want of principle and its want of profile. The chin a little higher, dear. Style largely depends on the way the chin is worn. They are worn very high, just at present. Algernon!

ALGERNON *(coming over)* Yes, Aunt Augusta.

LADY BRACKNELL There are distinct social possibilities in Miss Cardew's profile.

ALGERNON *(kissing* CECILY*)* Cecily is the sweetest, dearest, prettiest girl in the whole world. And I don't care twopence about social possibilities.

LADY BRACKNELL Never speak disrespectfully of society, Algernon. Only people who can't get into it do that. *(Glares at them kissing, then puts on a forced smile, taps* ALGERNON *with her fan and says to* CECILY*)* Dear child, of course you know that Algernon has nothing but his debts to depend on. But I do not approve of mercenary marriages. When I married Lord Bracknell I had no fortune of any kind. But I never dreamed for a moment of letting that stand in my way... Well, I suppose I must give my consent.

ALGERNON Thank you, Aunt Augusta.

LADY BRACKNELL Cecily, you may kiss me!

CECILY *(kisses her)* Thank you, Lady Bracknell.

LADY BRACKNELL You may also address me as Aunt Augusta for the future.

CECILY Thank you, Aunt Augusta.

LADY BRACKNELL The marriage, I think, had better take place quite soon.

ALGERNON Thank you, Aunt Augusta.

CECILY Thank you Aunt, Augusta.

LADY BRACKNELL To speak frankly, I am not in favour of long engagements. They give people the opportunity of finding out their true characters before marriage, which I think is never advisable.

JACK I beg your pardon for interrupting you, Lady Bracknell. But this engagement is quite out of the question. I am Miss Cardew's guardian. She cannot marry without my consent until she comes of age. That consent I absolutely decline to give.

LADY BRACKNELL Upon what grounds, may I ask? Algernon is an extremely, I may almost say an ostentatiously eligible young man. To my own knowledge he is on the list of nearly all the mothers in London.

JACK It pains me very much to have to speak frankly to you, Lady Bracknell, about your nephew, but the fact is that I do not approve at all of his moral character. I suspect him of being untruthful.

ALGERNON *and* **CECILY** *look at him in amazement.*

LADY BRACKNELL   Untruthful! My nephew Algernon? Impossible!

JACK I fear there can be no possible doubt about the matter. This morning at half past twelve, during my temporary absence in London on important business, he obtained admission into my house by means of the false pretence of being my brother. Under an assumed name he drank an entire pint bottle of my '74 champagne, a wine I was specially reserving for myself. Continuing his disgraceful deception he succeeded in the course of the afternoon in alienating the affections of my only ward. He subsequently stayed to tea and devoured every single muffin. And what makes his conduct all the more heartless is that he was perfectly well aware from the first that I have no brother, and that I never had a brother, not even of any kind. I distinctly told him so myself yesterday afternoon.

CECILY But, dear Uncle Jack, for the last year you have been telling us all that you had a brother. You dwelt continually on the subject. Algy merely corroborated your statement. It was noble of him.

JACK Pardon me, Cecily, you are a little too young to understand these matters. To invent anything at all is an act of sheer genius, and, in a commercial age like ours, shows considerable physical courage. Few of our modern novelists ever dare to invent a single thing. It is an open secret that they don't know how to do it. Upon the other hand, to corroborate a falsehood is a distinctly cowardly action. I know it is a thing that the newspapers do one for the other, every day. But it is not the act of a gentleman. No gentleman ever corroborates anything.

ALGERNON (*furiously*) Upon my word, Jack!

LADY BRACKNELL   Ahem! Mr Worthing, after careful consideration I have decided to overlook entirely my nephew's conduct to you, painful though it has been.

JACK That is very generous of you, Lady Bracknell. My own decision, however, is unalterable. I decline to give my consent.

LADY BRACKNELL (*to* CECILY) Come here, sweet child. (CECILY *goes over*) How old are you, dear?

CECILY Well, I am really only eighteen, but I always admit to twenty when I go to evening parties.

LADY BRACKNELL You are perfectly right in making some slight alteration. Indeed, nowhere and under no circumstances should a woman ever be quite accurate about her age. It looks so calculating... (*In a meditative manner*) Eighteen but admitting to twenty at evening parties. Well, whichever date you choose, dear, it will not be very long before you are of age and free from the restraints of tutelage. So I don't think that your guardian's consent to this alliance is, after all, a matter of much, if any, importance.

JACK Pray excuse me, Lady Bracknell, for interrupting you again, but it is only fair to tell you that according to the terms of her grandfather's will Miss Cardew does not come legally of age till she is thirty-five.

LADY BRACKNELL That does not seem to me a grave objection. Thirty-five is a very attractive age. London society is full of women of the very highest birth who have, of their own free choice, remained thirty-five for years. Lady Dumbleton is an instance in point. To my own knowledge she has been thirty-five ever since she arrived at the age of forty, which was many years ago now. And Lady Dumbleton is very much admired in the evening. I see no reason why our dear Cecily should not be even still more attractive at the age you mention than she is now. There will be large accumulation of property.

CECILY *(to* JACK*)* You are quite sure that I can't marry without your consent till I am thirty-five?

JACK That is the wise provision of your grandfather's will, Cecily. He undoubtedly foresaw the sort of difficulty that would be likely to occur.

CECILY Then grandpapa must have had a very extraordinary imagination. Algy...could you wait for me till I was thirty-five? Don't speak hastily. It is a very serious question, and much of my future happiness, as well as all of yours, depends upon your answer.

ALGERNON Of course I could, Cecily. How can you ask me such a question? I could wait for ever for you. You know I could.

CECILY Yes, I felt it instinctively. And I am so sorry for you, Algy. Because I couldn't wait all that time. I hate waiting even five minutes for anybody. It always makes me rather cross. I am not punctual myself, I know, but I do like punctuality in others, and waiting even to be married is quite out of the question. The very smallest delay often makes me a little irritable.

ALGERNON Then what is to be done, Cecily?

CECILY I don't know.

LADY BRACKNELL My dear Mr Worthing, as Miss Cardew states positively that she cannot wait till she is thirty-five—a remark which, I am bound to say, seems to me to show a somewhat impatient nature—I would beg of you to reconsider your decision.

JACK But, my dear Lady Bracknell, the matter is entirely in your own hands. The moment you consent to my marriage with Gwendolen, I will most gladly allow your nephew to form an alliance with my ward.

LADY BRACKNELL *(drawing herself up)* Mr Worthing, you must be quite aware that what you propose is out of the question.

JACK Then a passionate and careful celibacy is all that any of us can look forward to.

LADY BRACKNELL That is not the destiny I propose for Gwendolen. Algernon, of course, can choose for himself. *(Pulls out her watch.)* Come, dear, we have already missed five, if not six, trains. To miss any more might expose us to comment on the platform.

Enter **DR CHASUBLE** *from the garden.*

DR CHASUBLE Everything is quite ready for the christenings! I have been waiting in the church porch for now nearly half an hour.

LADY BRACKNELL The christenings, sir! Is not that somewhat premature?

DR CHASUBLE *(looking rather pulled and pointing to* **JACK** *and* **ALGERNON***)* Both these gentlemen have expressed a desire for immediate baptism.

LADY BRACKNELL At their age? The idea is grotesque and irreligious! *(To* **ALGERNON***)* Algernon, I forbid you to be baptised, I will not hear of such excesses. Lord Bracknell would be highly displeased if he learned that that was the way in which you wasted your time and money.

DR CHASUBLE Am I to understand then, that there are to be no baptisms at all this afternoon?

JACK I don't think that as things now stand it would be of any practical value to either of us, Dr Chasuble.

DR CHASUBLE I am grieved to hear such sentiments from you, Mr Worthing. They savour of the heretical views of the Anabaptists, views that I have completely refuted in four of my unpublished sermons. Baptismal regeneration is not to be lightly spoken of. Indeed, by the unanimous opinion of the fathers, baptism is a form of new birth. However, where adults are concerned, compulsory christening, except in the case of savage tribes, is, I regret to say, uncanonical, so I shall return to the church at once. Indeed, I have just been informed by the pew-opener that for the last hour and a half Miss Prism has been waiting for me in the vestry.

LADY BRACKNELL *(starting)* Miss Prism! Did I hear you mention a Miss Prism?

DR CHASUBLE Yes, Lady Bracknell. I am on my way to join her.

LADY BRACKNELL *(anxiously)* Pray allow me to detain you for a moment. This matter may prove to be one of vital importance to Lord Bracknell and myself. Is this Miss Prism a female of repellent aspect, remotely connected with education?

DR CHASUBLE *(somewhat indignant)* She is the most cultivated of ladies, and the very picture of respectability.

LADY BRACKNELL *(thoughtfully)* It is obviously the same person. May I ask what position she holds in your household?

DR CHASUBLE *(severely)* I am a celibate, madam.

JACK *(interposing)* Miss Prism, Lady Bracknell, has been for the last three years Miss Cardew's esteemed governess and companion.

LADY BRACKNELL Then let me strongly advise you, Mr Worthing, should she turn out to be the person I suspect her of being, never to allow her under any circumstances to take Miss Cardew out in a perambulator. The result might be lamentable. I must see this Miss Prism at once. Let her be sent for.

DR CHASUBLE *(looking off)* She approaches—she is here.

Enter MISS PRISM *hurriedly.*

MISS PRISM I was told you expected me in the vestry, dear Canon. I have been waiting for you there for an hour and three quarters. *(Catches sight of* LADY BRACKNELL *who has fixed her with a stony glare.* MISS PRISM *grows pale and quails. She looks anxiously round as if desirous to escape)*

LADY BRACKNELL *(in a severe judicial voice)* Prism!!

MISS PRISM *bows her head in shame.*

Come here, Prism!

MISS PRISM *approaches in a humble manner.*

Prism! Where is that baby?

*General consternation—*DR CHASUBLE *starts back in horror.* ALGERNON *and* JACK *pretend to be anxious to shield* CECILY *and* GWEHDOLEU *from hearing a terrible scandal—*MISS PRISM *makes no answer.*

Twenty-eight years ago, Prism, you left Lord Bracknell's house, number 104 Upper Grosvenor Street, in charge of a permabulator that contained a baby of the male sex. You never returned. A few weeks later, through the elaborate investigation of the Metropolitan police, the perambulator was discovered at midnight standing by itself in a remote corner of Hyde Park. It contained the manuscript of a three-volume novel of more than usually revolting sentimentality.

MISS PRISM *starts in involuntary indignation.*

But the baby was not there.

Everyone looks at MISS PRISM.

Prism! Where is that baby?

A pause.

MISS PRISM Lady Bracknell, I admit with shame that I do not know. I only wish I did. The plain facts of the case are these. On the morning of the day you mention, a day that is for ever branded in my memory, I prepared, as usual, to take the baby out in its perambulator. I had also with me a somewhat old, but capacious handbag in which I intended to place the manuscript of a three-volume novel that I had written during my few unoccupied hours. In a moment of mental abstraction, for which I never can forgive myself,

I deposited the manuscript in the bassinet, and placed the baby in the handbag.

JACK *(who has been listening attentively)* But where did you deposit the handbag?

MISS PRISM Do not ask me, Mr Worthing.

JACK Miss Prism, this is a matter of no small importance to me. I insist on knowing where you deposited the handbag that contained the infant.

MISS PRISM I left it, Mr Worthing, in the cloak-room of one of the large railway-stations in London.

JACK What railway station?

MISS PRISM *(quite crushed)* Victoria. The Brighton Line.

LADY BRACKNELL *(looking at JACK)* I sincerely hope nothing improbable is going to happen. The improbable is always in bad, or at any rate, questionable taste.

JACK I must retire to my bedroom for a moment.

DR CHASUBLE This news seems to have upset you, Mr Worthing. I trust your indisposition is merely temporary.

JACK I will be back in a few moments, dear Canon. Gwendolen! Wait here for me!

GWENDOLEN If you are not too long, I will wait here for you all my life.

Exit JACK *in great excitement.*

DR CHASUBLE What do you think this means, Lady Bracknell?

LADY BRACKNELL I dare not even suspect, Dr Chasuble. I need hardly tell you that in families of high position strange coincidences are not supposed to occur. They are hardly considered the thing.

Noise heard overhead as if someone was throwing trunks about. Everyone looks up.

CECILY *(looking up)* Uncle Jack seems strangely agitated.

DR CHASUBLE Your guardian has a very emotional nature.

LADY BRACKNELL The noise is extremely unpleasant. It sounds as if he was having an argument with the furniture. I dislike arguments of any kind. They are always vulgar, and usually violent.

DR CHASUBLE *(looking up)* It has stopped now.

Loud bang overhead.

CECILY No, it has begun again.

LADY BRACKNELL I wish he would arrive at some conclusion.

GWENDOLEN This suspense is terrible. I hope it will last.

Enter JACK with a handbag of black leather in his hand.

JACK *(rushing over to MISS PRISM)* Is this the handbag, Miss Prism? *(Hands it to her)* Examine it carefully before you speak. The happiness of more than one life depends on your answer.

MISS PRISM *(puts on her spectacles)* It seems to be mine. Yes, here is the injury it received through the upsetting of a Gower Street omnibus in younger and happier days. *(Opens bag)* Here is the indelible stain left on the lining by the accidental explosion of a temperance beverage, an incident that occurred at Leamington. *(In a more confident and joyful voice)* Yes, and here on the lock are my initials. I had forgotten that I had had them placed there. The bag is undoubtedly mine. I am delighted to have it so unexpectedly restored to me. It has been a great inconvenience being without it all these years.

JACK *(in a pathetic voice)* But Miss Prism, more is restored to you than the handbag. I was the baby you placed in it.

MISS PRISM *(amazed)* You?

JACK *(embracing her)* Yes...mother!

MISS PRISM *(recoiling in indignant astonishment)* Mr Worthing, I am unmarried!

JACK Unmarried! I do not deny that that is a serious blow. But after all, who has the right to throw a stone against one who has suffered? Cannot repentance wipe out an act of folly? Why should there be one law for men and another for women? Mother! I forgive you. *(Tries to embrace her again)*

MISS PRISM *(still more indignant)* But Mr Worthing, there is some error. Maternity has never been an incident in my life. The suggestion, if it were not made before such a large number of people, would be almost indelicate. *(Pointing to* LADY BRACKNELL*)* There stands the lady who can tell you who you really are. *(Retires to back of stage)*

JACK *(after a pause)* Lady Bracknell, I hate to seem inquisitive, but would you kindly inform me who I am?

LADY BRACKNELL I am afraid that the news I have to give you will not altogether please you. You are the son of my poor sister, Mrs Moncrieff, and consequently Algernon's elder brother.

JACK Algy's elder brother. Then I have a brother after all! I knew I had a brother! I always said I had a brother. Cecily— how could you have ever doubted that I had a brother? Dr Chasuble, my unfortunate brother. Miss Prism, my unfortunate brother. Gwendolen, my unfortunate brother. *(Seizes hold of* ALGERNON*)* Algy, you young scoundrel, you will have to treat me with more respect in the future. You have never behaved to me like a brother in all your life.

ALGERNON Well, not till to-day, old boy, I admit. *(Shakes hands)* I did my best, however, though I was out of practice.

GWENDOLEN *(to* JACK*)* Darling!

JACK Darling!

LADY BRACKNELL Under these strange and unforeseen circumstances you can kiss your Aunt Augusta.

JACK *(staying where he is)* I am dazed with happiness. *(Kisses* GWENDOLEN*)* I hardly know who I am kissing.

ALGERNON *takes opportunity to kiss* CECILY.

GWENDOLEN I hope that will be the last time I shall ever hear you make such an observation.

JACK It will, darling.

MISS PRISM *(advancing, after coughing slightly)* Mr Worthing,— Mr Moncrieff as I should call you now—after what has just occurred I feel it my duty to resign my position in this household. Any inconvenience I may have caused you in your infancy through placing you inadvertently in this handbag I sincerely apologise for.

JACK Don't mention it, dear Miss Prism. Don't mention anything. I am sure I had a very pleasant time in your nice handbag in spite of the slight damage it received through the overturning of an omnibus in your happier days. As for leaving us, the suggestion is absurd.

MISS PRISM It is my duty to leave. I have really nothing more to teach dear Cecily. In the very difficult accomplishment of getting married I fear my sweet and clever pupil has far outstripped her teacher.

DR CHASUBLE A moment—Laetitia!

MISS PRISM Dr Chasuble!

DR CHASUBLE Laetitia, I have come to the conclusion that the Primitive Church was in error on certain points. Corrupt readings seem to have crept into the text. I beg to solicit the honour of your hand.

MISS PRISM Frederick, at the present moment words fail me to express my feelings. But I will forward you, this evening, the three last volumes of my diary. In these you will be able to peruse a full account of the sentiments that I have entertained towards you for the last eighteen months.

Enter MERRIMAN.

MERRIMAN Lady Bracknell's flyman says he cannot wait any longer.

LADY BRACKNELL *(rising)* True! I must return to town at once. *(Pulls out watch)* I see I have now missed no less than nine trains. There is only one more.

Exit **MERRIMAN**—**LADY BRACKNELL** *moves towards the door.*

Prism, from your last observation to Dr Chasuble, I learn with regret that you have not yet given up your ridiculously sentimental passion for fiction in three volumes. And, if you really are going to enter into the state of matrimony which at your age seems to me, I feel bound to say, rather like flying in the face of an all-wise Providence, I trust you will be more careful of your husband than you were of your infant charge, and not leave poor Dr Chasuble lying about at railway stations in handbags or receptacles of any kind. Cloak-rooms are notoriously draughty places.

MISS PRISM *bows her head meekly.*

Dr Chasuble, you have my sincere good wishes, and if baptism be, as you say it is, a form of new birth, I would strongly advise you to have Miss Prism baptised without delay. To be born again would be of considerable advantage to her. Whether such a procedure be in accordance with the practice of the Primitive Church I do not know. But it is hardly probable, I should fancy, that they had to grapple with such extremely advanced problems. *(Turning sweetly to* **CECILY** *and patting her cheek)* Sweet child! We will expect you at Upper Grosvenor Street in a few days.

CECILY Thank you, Aunt Augusta!

LADY BRACKNELL Come, Gwendolen.

GWENDOLEN *(to* **JACK***)* My own! But what own are you? What is your Christian name, now that you have become someone else?

JACK Good heavens! ...I had quite forgotten that point. Your decision on the subject of my name is irrevocable, I suppose?

GWENDOLEN I never change, except in my affections.

CECILY What a noble nature you have, Gwendolen.

JACK Then the question had better be cleared up at once. Aunt Augusta, a moment. At the time when Miss Prism left me in the handbag, had I been christened already? Pray be calm, Aunt Augusta. This is a terrible crisis and much depends on your answer.

LADY BRACKNELL (*quite calmly*) Every luxury that money could buy, including christening, had been lavished on you by your fond and doting parents.

JACK Then I was christened? That is settled. Now what name was I given? Let me know the worst.

LADY BRACKNELL (*after a pause*) Being the eldest son you were naturally christened after your father. I distinctly remember your being christened after your father.

JACK (*irritably*) Yes, but what was my father's Christian name? Pray don't be so calm, Aunt Augusta. This is a terrible crisis and everything hangs on the nature of your reply. What was my father's Christian name?

LADY BRACKNELL (*meditatively*) I cannot at the present moment recall what the General's Christian name was. Your poor dear mother always addressed him as "General". That I remember perfectly. Indeed, I don't think she would have dared to have called him by his Christian name. But I have no doubt he had one. He was violent in his manner, but there was nothing eccentric about him in any way. That was the result of the Indian climate, and marriage, and indigestion, and other things of that kind. In fact he was rather a martinet about the little details of daily life. Too much so, I used to tell my sister.

JACK (*to* ALGERNON) Algy! Can't you recollect what our father's Christian name was?

ALGERNON My dear boy, we never were on those sort of terms. Indeed, I don't think we can ever have been even on speaking terms. He died, I believe, before I was a year old.

JACK *(agitated and impressive)* His name would appear in the Army Lists of the period, I suppose, Aunt Augusta?

LADY BRACKNELL The General was essentially a man of peace, except in his domestic life. But I have no doubt his name would appear in any military directory.

JACK The Army Lists of the last forty years are here. *(Pointing to bookcase)* I see now how foolish I have been to neglect them for more trivial works like books on agriculture, treatises on bimetallism, and novels with a purpose. *(Rushes to bookcase and tears the books out. Distributing them rapidly)* Here, Dr Chasuble—Miss Prism, two for you—Cecily, Cecily, an Army List. Make a précis of it at once. Algernon, pray search English history for our father's Christian name if you have the smallest filial affection left. Aunt Augusta, I beg you to bring your masculine mind to bear on this subject. Gwendolen—no, it would agitate you too much. Leave these researches to less philosophic natures like ours.

GWENDOLEN *(heroically)* Give me six copies of any period, this century or the last. I do not care which!

JACK Noble girl! Here are a dozen. More might be an inconvenience to you. *(Brings her a pile of Army Lists— rushes through them himself taking each one from her hands as she tries to examine it)* No, just let me look. No, allow me, dear. Darling, I think I can find it out sooner. Just allow me, my love.

DR CHASUBLE What station, Mr Moncrieff, did you say you wished to go to?

JACK *(pausing in despair)* Station! Who on earth is talking about a station? I merely want to find out my father's Christian name.

DR CHASUBLE But you have handed me a Bradshaw. *(Looks at it)* Of 1869, I observe. A book of considerable antiquarian interest: but not in any way bearing on the question of the names usually conferred on Generals at baptism.

CECILY I am so sorry, Uncle Jack. But Generals don't seem to be even alluded to in the "History of our own times", although it is the best edition. The one written in collaboration with the typewriting machine.

MISS PRISM To me, Mr Moncrieff, you have given two copies of the Price Lists of the Civil Service Stores. I do not find Generals marked anywhere. There seems to be either no demand or no supply.

LADY BRACKNELL This treatise, the "Green Carnation", as I see it is called, seems to be a book about the culture of exotics. It contains no reference to Generals in it. It seems a morbid and middle-class affair.

JACK *(very irritable indeed, to* ALGERNON*)* Good Heavens! And what nonsense are you reading, Algy? *(Takes book from him)* The Army List? Well, I don't suppose you knew it was the Army List. And you've got it open at the wrong page. Besides, there is the thing staring you in the face. M. Generals... Mallam—what ghastly names they have— Markby, Migsby, Mobbs, Moncrieff, Moncrieff! Lieutenant 1840, Captain, Lieutenant-Colonel, Colonel, General 1860. Christian names, Ernest John. *(Puts book very quietly down and speaks quite calmly)* I always told you, Gwendolen, my name was Ernest, didn't I? Well, it is Ernest after all. I mean it naturally is Ernest.

LADY BRACKNELL Yes, I remember now that the General was called Ernest. I knew I had some particular reason for disliking the name. Come, Gwendolen.

Exit LADY BRACKNELL.

GWENDOLEN Ernest! My own Ernest! I felt from the first that you could have had no other name. Even all man's useless information, wonderful though it is, is nothing compared to the instinct of a good woman.

JACK Gwendolen, it is a terrible thing for a man to find out suddenly that all his life he has been speaking nothing but the truth. Can you forgive me?

GWENDOLEN I can. For I feel that you are sure to change. There is always hope even for those who are most accurate in their statements.

JACK My own one!

DR CHASUBLE Laetitia! *(Embraces her)*

ALGERNON Cecily! *(Embraces her)*

JACK Gwendolen! *(Embraces her)*

Enter **LADY BRACKNELL.**

LADY BRACKNELL I have missed the last train! —My nephew, you seem to be displaying signs of triviality.

JACK On the contrary, Aunt Augusta, I've now realised for the first time in my life the vital Importance of Being Earnest.

Tableaux.

Curtain.

FURNITURE AND PROPERTY LIST

ACT I

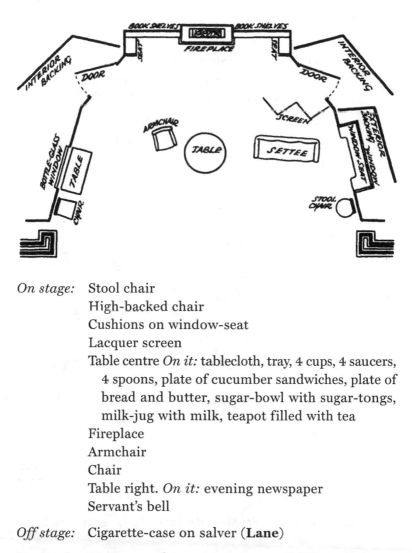

On stage: Stool chair
High-backed chair
Cushions on window-seat
Lacquer screen
Table centre *On it:* tablecloth, tray, 4 cups, 4 saucers, 4 spoons, plate of cucumber sandwiches, plate of bread and butter, sugar-bowl with sugar-tongs, milk-jug with milk, teapot filled with tea
Fireplace
Armchair
Chair
Table right. *On it:* evening newspaper
Servant's bell

Off stage: Cigarette-case on salver (**Lane**)

Personal: Visiting card in note-case, pencil (**Algernon**)
Pencil and note-book (**Lady Bracknell**)

ACT II

On stage: Table. *On it:* books, **Cecily**'s diary, pen and ink
              2 garden chairs
              Wicker chair
              Wooden seat

Offstage: Watering-pot (**Cecily**)
              Card on salver (**Merriman**)
              Second card on salver (**Merriman**)
              Large folio containing papers (**Gribsby**)

Personal: Pink roses round waist (**Cecily**)
              Note-pad and pencil (**Dr Chasuble**)
              Watch (**Gribsby**)

ACT III

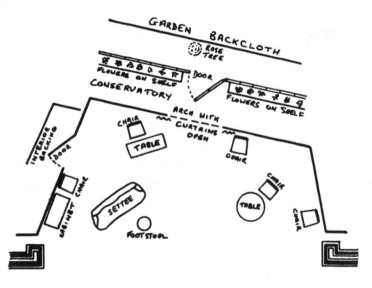

On stage: Table 1. *On it:* **Miss Prism**'s diary, pencil and large
              hat
              5 chairs
              Settee
              Footstool

Cabinet. *In it:* books

Table (with drawer). *On it:* **Cecily**'s diary, pen and ink, box containing letters tied up with blue ribbon

Offstage: Tablecloth, plate of bread and butter, salver (**Merriman**)

Tray. *On it:* 4 cups, 4 saucers, sugar-bowl with tongs, milk-jug with milk, teapot (**Footman**)

Cake-stand with uncut cake and knife, muffins, tea-cake (**Footman**)

Personal: Ring, gold bangle, pearl necklace (**Cecily**)

Watch (**Algernon**)

Lorgnette, diary, (**Gwendolen**)

ACT IV

On stage: As Act III

Offstage: Black leather hand-bag (JACK)

Personal: Watch, fan (**Lady Bracknell**)

Spectacles (**Miss Prism**)

LIGHTING PLOT

ACT I Summer afternoon

To open: Full general lighting in Algernon's rooms
          No cues.

ACT II July afternoon

To open: Effect of bright sunshine
          No cues.

ACT III July afternoon

To open: Full general lighting in sitting-room
          No cues.

ACT IV July afternoon
As ACT III

EFFECTS PLOT
ACT I

Cue 1   As Curtain rises   (Page 1)
Piano playing off. Cut music just before
Algernon *enters.*

Cue 2   **Algernon**: "... listen attentively."   (Page 11)
Bell ring off right.

Cue 3   **Lady Bracknell** exits   (Page 21)
"THE WEDDING MARCH" played on
the piano off left.

Cue 4   **Jack**: "...that ghastly tune, Algy."   (Page 22)
Piano playing stops.

ACT II
No cues.

ACT III
No cues.

ACT IV

Cue 5   **Lady Bracknell**: "...considered the thing." (Page 92)
Loud thuds and hangings overhead.

Cue 6   **Lady Bracknell**: "...usually, violent." (Page 93)
Overhead noises stop.

Cue 7   **Dr Chasuble**: "It has stopped now." (Page 93)
Loud bang overhead.

VISIT THE
SAMUEL FRENCH
BOOKSHOP
AT THE
ROYAL COURT THEATRE

Browse plays and theatre books, get expert advice and enjoy a coffee

Samuel French Bookshop
Royal Court Theatre
Sloane Square
London
SW1W 8AS
020 7565 5024

Shop from thousands of titles on our website

 samuelfrench.co.uk

 samuelfrenchltd

samuel french uk

CPSIA information can be obtained
at www.ICGtesting.com
Printed in the USA
LVHW080451140122
708525LV00019B/2257

9 780573 111983